SHOPACHECK'S
RUGBY LEAGUE
REVIEW
1985

SHOPACHECK'S RUGBY LEAGUE REVIEW 1985

faber and faber

LONDON · BOSTON

First published in 1985
by Faber and Faber Limited
3 Queen Square London WC1N 3AU

Photoset and printed in Great Britain by
Redwood Burn Limited
Trowbridge, Wiltshire

British Library Cataloguing in Publication Data

Shopacheck's Rugby League Review 1985.
1. Rugby football—Periodicals
796.33′3′05   GV944.8

ISBN 0–571–13687–7
ISBN 0–571–13690–7 Pbk
ISSN 0267–8454

Library of Congress Cataloging in Publication Data

Shopacheck's Rugby League Review 1985.
1. Rugby football—Tournaments.   I. Title.
GV945.5.F58   1985   796.33′374   85–12852
ISBN 0–571–13687–7
ISBN 0–571–13690–7 (pbk.)

Contents

Acknowledgements

For permission to include photographs the publisher's thanks
are due to the following agencies:
D. Bradbury (25)
The Reporter Series Ltd (26)
Eddie Rolmanis (5, 18–19, 22)
Andrew Varley Picture Agency (1–4, 6–17, 20–21, 23–24, 27–
31).

1

THE INTERNATIONAL SEASON

During the 1984–85 season control of the Great Britain side passed from Frank Myler and Dick Gemmell to Maurice Bamford and Les Bettinson. Myler, with unfortunate timing, had announced midway through Britain's tour of Australasia that he was not seeking to extend his term as British coach but would be taking over as general manager at Oldham; while Gemmell, who had managed that unsuccessful tour, went back to Australia after a brief return to England.

Bamford was selected from a short list of six. He was an interesting choice because he had enjoyed neither the success as a coach nor as a player that some of his rivals for the job – Malcolm Reilly, Roger Millward, Allan Agar, Peter Fox, and Arthur Bunting – had. He had spent three months at Dewsbury in 1974, been assistant to Peter Fox at Bradford and then had two productive years at Halifax, where good husbandry helped to give a destitute club some much needed success. A year at Huddersfield ended in a deal of bitterness and a year at Wigan with the sack. He then had a spell at Bramley, but his fortunes declined so badly that he drifted out of the professional game, though continuing to give the amateur side Oulton Welfare the benefit of his experience.

Leeds revived his career by appointing him successor to Robin Dewhurst. It was a job that Bamford could not have dreamed of filling but he grasped his unexpected opportunity gratefully. His appointment coincided with the start of a long unbeaten run by Leeds who went on, splendidly, to beat Widnes in the final of the John Player Trophy.

Of the six men on the short list Bamford was the outsider, but in his favour was an infectious enthusiasm and a reputation for straight-talking, honesty and loyalty. His occupation as a self-employed builder seemed an apt job for a man about to reconstruct the international team. Bamford's appointment was announced to the gathered media at Chapeltown Road in October and his first press conference was impressive. He generated a feeling that Britain was about to embark on a programme that would be characterized by a collective sense of purpose. As Bamford outlined his plans for the future his chief theme was that everyone in the game must work towards a common cause. 'I want to stress that this is a team job. It is too big for one man and I will need all the help I can get from all the other coaches and chairmen and from everyone involved in the game,' he said.

Bamford asserted his belief that Britain's future lay in the hands of the young. The game no longer belonged to '19-stone dinosaurs'. There had never been as many good young players, with the operative word 'young', he said, as there were at present. Practically every club, first and second division, had at least one potential international. 'As I see it, we need to cream off these players and bring them together in an environment where they will train together regularly and in which every man knows that he will have the opportunity to pull on a Great Britain jersey. These players need to be taken away from the old mercenaries and instructed and educated in the importance of the two prime disciplines ... self and team.' It would be hard to find serious fault with that philosophy.

So, after outlining his ambitions and plans, what sort of a season did Bamford eventually look back on? As far as results were concerned, it was largely successful. His Under-21 sides beat the French at Castleford and at Albi. In the full Tests Great Britain ran in a record number of points against France at Leeds but lost the return at Perpignan a fortnight later, while the Colts side, though not directly his responsibility, drew at Mazamet and won at Craven Park, Hull. The two Under-21 games were disappointing although Bamford, perhaps motivated by a sense of loyalty to his players, was able to see qualities in those games that eluded less perceptive critics. He did, though, concede that the game at Albi was 'very dull and very boring'. But he had every right to feel elated at his side's performance in the first Test at Headingley, where his players gave a rewarding example of sustained, enterprising, attacking rugby.

Bamford was criticized – as any national coach is likely to be. He perhaps made mistakes – as coaches will. But Bamford, who admitted when he took the job that he was not afraid of being exposed to new ideas, seemed to have a clear knowledge of what he was trying to achieve, even if this was not always appreciated by some of the doubters. The chief criticism of his squads for the two major internationals, the Tests at Leeds and Perpignan, was that they excluded a number of obviously good players. Bamford was thus accused of not selecting his best team and, by not doing so, of devaluing Test football. Bamford, not the first man to do so, had come across that old, intractable problem of lack of international opportunities.

Nevertheless the two Tests, particularly the one lost by Britain in

Perpignan, were instructive, which is what Bamford wanted them to be. The Leeds Test showed him that he was working with some promising – and in the cases of Hanley and Goodway, outstanding – material; Perpignan showed that certain players were not good enough, or not yet ready, for Test football. It must have been disappointing for Bamford to endure defeat after his side had played so well at Headingley, but at least he was now more aware of the capabilities of a larger number of players, and could be commended unreservedly on the near faultless discipline shown by his men in both Tests.

The 1984–85 season was directed towards one objective: to produce a squad from which would come the Test side to meet New Zealand in 1985–86. After the game in Perpignan, Bamford and Les Bettinson, who had been appointed manager in February, Phil Larder, the director of the National Coaching Scheme, and Rod McKenzie, the fitness expert from Carnegie College, met to select a squad that would prepare for that series throughout the summer.

They emerged with one necessarily larger than intended because nine players were to spend the summer playing in Australia. Of those nine, Goodway, Schofield, Drummond and Hanley were almost assured of places in the Test side while the other five, Rathbone, Crooks, Harkin, Noble and Divorty, were likely to be powerful contenders. In the event, Hanley, Drummond, Divorty and Rathbone did not go to Australia. But at the time it was accepted that, for training-on purposes, a squad of seventeen would not have been big enough, and so a panel of twenty-eight plus the Australia-bound players was named, giving a total of thirty-seven.

Three players, much to the disappointment of Bamford, made themselves unavailable. Tony Myler, of Widnes, and Andy Gregory, now with Warrington, asked to be excused for business reasons while Garry Clark, the teenage Hull KR winger, felt after two successive tours of Australia that he needed a rest. Bamford felt no sympathy towards them and publicly aired his displeasure. Ronnie Duane, the young Warrington centre, also asked to be excused, but that was because he was still trying to recover full fitness after suffering a bad knee injury in Australia the year before. The squad was:

Full-backs: Mick Burke (Widnes), George Fairbairn (Hull KR), Chris Johnson (Leigh)

Wings: Des Drummond (Leigh), Joe Lydon (Widnes), Phil Ford (Wigan), Henderson Gill (Wigan), Barry Ledger (St Helens)

Centres: Garry Schofield (Hull), Vince Gribbin (Whitehaven), Ellery Hanley (Bradford Northern), David Creasser (Leeds), David Stephenson (Wigan), Kieron O'Loughlin (Widnes)

Half-backs: Steve Peters (St Helens), Shaun Edwards (Wigan), Deryck Fox (Featherstone Rovers), Paul Harkin (Hull KR), Bob Beardmore (Castleford)

11

Props: Lee Crooks (Hull), Roy Dickinson (Leeds), Tony Burke (St Helens), Mike O'Neill (Widnes), Andy Goodway (Oldham), Andy Dannatt (Hull)

Hookers: Kevin Beardmore (Castleford), David Watkinson (Hull KR), Brian Noble (Bradford Northern)

Second-row: David Hobbs (Oldham), Alan Rathbone (Bradford Northern), Ian Potter (Wigan), John Fieldhouse (Widnes), Chris Burton (Hull KR), Andy Platt (St Helens)

Loose forwards: Gary Divorty (Hull), Chris Arkwright (St Helens), Harry Pinner (St Helens)

Eugene Cross Park, Ebbw Vale, 14 October
Wales 9   England 28

This international, played in the heartland of Rugby Union, was arguably a misconceived idea that turned out better than anticipated. Although bolstered by such experienced players as Skerrett, Prendiville, Shaw and Juliff, and possessing genuine talent in Wilson and Phil Ford, Wales, by any yardstick, fielded a weak side. Six of their players came from the newly-formed Bridgend club which was to secure only one league victory all season. A dispute at Fulham had deprived David Watkins, the Welsh team manager, of good players such as Cambriani, Bayliss, Diamond, Souto and Herdman and the occasion seemed likely to degenerate into the sort of senseless massacre witnessed on a broiling May day at St Helens in 1978.

After that match, Ronnie Simpson, the Welsh team manager, had aired doubts regarding Wales's continued existence as a Rugby League nation. But, however tenuously, they had survived and now Watkins was prepared to defend this contest against its many detractors. 'Our international football is too limited. Rugby League has been domiciled only in the north for ninety years. Unless it spreads it has no future,' he said. But what point is there in international football when the sides are so patently mismatched? International caps should be earned. The public will not be fooled by such games. So ran some of the counter-arguments, and a lowly attendance of 2,111 would seem to question the wisdom of such a match.

Nevertheless, Watkins was vindicated. Wales acquitted themselves far better than expected and although the crowd was disappointingly small the match proved to be not simply a lively, entertaining contest but a worthwhile exercise in public relations, helped by being given full coverage on Welsh television. The worst fears, though, seemed likely to be realized when after only twenty-four minutes Garry Clark, the Hull KR winger, had scored the three quickest tries of his career; and a rout was starting to take shape by half-time, at which point England led 22–0. The second half, however, surprised everybody, probably even the Welsh players themselves.

Danny Wilson, the Swinton stand-off, was the omnipotent figure of this second act. He had had a curious first half in which he had mixed skill with aberration, once throwing out an over-ambitious pass that was intercepted by Clark on his own '25', leaving him with a long, clear run to the opposition's posts. Now, Wilson's elusive running began to cause the England defence a lot of problems.

Wales had begun to show signs of retaliation towards the end of the first half and their revival really gained momentum when Wilson, in the forty-sixth minute, dummied his way through the first line of defence and then with a swivel of his hips sent Burke, the England full-back, lurching the wrong way. His touchdown gave Hallett an easy kick at goal.

Encouraged, the Welsh went in search of more points and earned them through a penalty by Hallett and a drop goal by Wilson. But that was as much as Wales could manage. Juliff had departed with a broken arm in the first half, and now Wilson, who played with his thigh heavily strapped and had been advised by Swinton not to take part in the game, left the field. McJennett and Skerrett increasingly began to feel the injuries they had been carrying.

Not surprisingly Wales began to tire and towards the end, from one of twelve scrums out of thirteen won by England, Burke ran clear to score England's fifth try. The same player added the goal points and England now had an advantage of 19 points but between England's fourth and fifth tries thirty-seven minutes had elapsed. It had been a period of commendable Welsh spirit.

The game probably did less for English reputations than for Welsh; Wilson and Ford especially had fine games. But even in a contest of limited significance, Andy Goodway's exceptional talents were again obvious while Hanley's long-range try of the first half showed this exciting player at his best.

Wales: Hallett (Bridgend); Camilleri (Bridgend), Prendiville (Hull), Davies (Bridgend), Ford (Warrington); Wilson (Swinton), Flowers (Bridgend); Skerrett (Hull), Preece (Bradford Northern), Shaw (Wigan), McJennett (Barrow), O'Brien (Bridgend), Juliff (Wigan)

Substitutes: Walters (Bridgend) for Flowers after 27 minutes, Johns (Blackpool Borough) for Juliff after 31 minutes

Scorers: try – Wilson; goals – Hallett (2); drop goal – Wilson

13

England: Burke (Widnes); Drummond (Leigh), Schofield (Hull), Hanley (Bradford Northern), Clark (Hull KR); Donlan (Leigh), Cairns (Barrow); Hobbs (Featherstone Rovers), Kevin Beardmore (Castleford), Waddell (Blackpool Borough), Kelly (Hull KR), Goodway (Oldham), Huddart (Whitehaven)

Substitutes: Arkwright (St Helens) for Hobbs after 64 minutes, Ledger (St Helens) for Clark after 72 minutes

Scorers: tries – Clark (3), Hanley, Burke; goals – Burke (4)

Referee: D. W. Fox (Wakefield)

Attendance: 2,111

**Wheldon Road, Castleford, 25 November
Great Britain Under-21 24   France Under-21 8**

Even in prosperous times Castleford would have been an odd choice for this Under-21 international. To take the match there during the miners' strike was baffling, and it was no surprise that the attendance was only 1,754. While there is a valid argument for spreading international occasions, playing at Castleford when money was scarce and people's minds concentrated on more pressing issues was a misjudgment. The alternatives might have been Hull on the Friday night or Wigan on the Sunday. A conservative estimate suggested that the choice of Castleford had cost the game between £4,000 and £5,000. Maurice Bamford certainly would have preferred a more inviting setting, a less tepid atmosphere, in which to launch his career as British coach, though at least he did begin with a win.

Not that it was a particularly gratifying victory, but it did have the merit of being against older opponents. After a series of Under-24 internationals the age stipulation had been lowered by three years but the French ignored it. They would not, they claimed, have been able to field a side of Under-21 players. There was not, however, any sense of outrage or injustice in the British camp at this discrepancy in ages.

Possibly the most disappointing aspects of the British performance were the minimal contributions made by such established internationals as Schofield, Crooks and Clark, who showed too much pace for the French in the eighteenth minute when he scored the first of three British tries but then lapsed into anonymity. Schofield, who had earned so many plaudits on the previous summer's tour of Australasia, looked listless; Crooks laboured. All round, Britain gave a sound but unimaginative performance which was never going to set Wheldon Road alight.

It was a sign of the general level of mediocrity that a press panel, asked to choose the man of the match, had difficulty reaching a decision. In truth, any individual receiving the award would have been flattered, but it was given to Creasser, the Leeds stand-off, as much for his significant contribution of six goals than for any spectacular play.

If anything, Britain were too adventurous, a forgivable fault at least. They threw out a number of long passes that fell on barren ground, looking a more co-ordinated side when they opted for something less expansive but more efficient. Against that, their defence, in spite of a couple of lapses, was sound and their three tries were well taken.

After Creasser had given Britain the lead with a penalty in the sixth minute the French, to some surprise, took the lead seven minutes later. Edwards hesitated crucially in moving to his left to cover Rocci's high, probing kick and the French right wing, Bertheloite, moved in decisively for the touchdown. Clark, from Schofield's adept reverse pass, re-established British supremacy in the nineteenth minute and then, seven minutes later, the referee, M. Monzat, had a brawl to contend with.

The trouble erupted at a scrum and quickly two sizeable groups were involved in some vicious kicking and punching while play irrelevantly continued on the right side of the pitch. It was, briefly, a nasty loss of discipline, with Crooks singled out as the scapegoat and banished for ten minutes to the sin-bin. In spite of M. Monzat's bizarre control – even the French thought his use of the whistle excessive – there was nothing as serious again. The contest recovered its equilibrium and by half-time Britain led 10–4.

France were encouraged at the start of the second half as they had been at the start of the first and once again it was the kicking of Rocci that caused the problems. He pursued his downfield kick but was unable to gather the bouncing ball. Romano, up in support, could and although his touchdown looked a little dubious the score stood. Rocci, unable to add the goal points to Bertheloite's earlier try, was now unable to improve Romano's.

There followed Britain's best period of the afternoon. A broadly-based crossfield move involving Schofield, Edwards and Allen gave Currier the opportunity to race in at the left corner and, eleven minutes later, from a scrum twenty yards from the French line, Conway showed a keen sense of anticipation and a clean pair of heels, sprinting through the French defence to score.

Great Britain Under-21: Edwards (Wigan); Clark (Hull KR), Schofield (Hull), Allen (St Helens), Currier (Widnes); Creasser (Leeds), Conway (Leeds); Crooks (Hull), Groves (Salford), Dannatt (Hull), Round (St Helens), Powell (Leeds), Divorty (Hull)

Substitutes: Gribbin (Whitehaven) for Allen after 59 minutes, Proctor (Hull) for Round after 50 minutes

Scorers: tries – Clark, Currier, Conway; goals – Creasser (6)

France Under-21: Wosniack (Villefranche); Bertheloite (Toulouse), Bret (St Estève), Lapeyre (Albi), Martinez (Carpentras); Rocci (Le Pontet), Alberola (Lézignan); Haraca (St Estève), Batello (Carcassonne), Romano (Carpentras), Boulagnon (Villefranche), Cunac (Albi), Verde (Villeneuve)

Substitutes: Hurtado (Lézignan) for Batello after 61 minutes, Berge (Le Pontet) not used

Scorers: tries – Bertheloite, Romano

Referee: J–C Monzat (France)

Attendance: 1,754

Mazamet, 15 December
France Colts 14   Great Britain Colts 14

Great Britain opened this game enterprisingly at the pleasant little stadium at Mazamet and ended it pressing hard for victory. But it would have been an injustice if they had succeeded in a contest which, for a lengthy middle period, was notable for the imagination and quality of the French play.

A number of British officials among the crowd of 500 were highly critical of Fred Lindop's refereeing which they felt had heavily favoured the French. It was not the first time, of course, that a referee was held to blame for a disappointing result and such an obsession was especially galling on this occasion because it tended to obscure a central truth: which was that the French were by far the better side.

Superbly served by Espugna and Pech at half-back, by Vincent Baloup at full-back, Esponella and Calas in the centre, and by Brencz, Luchési and

16

Guasch in the forwards, the French handled the more skilfully, ran the more imaginatively and produced by far the better support play.

Britain, possibly fooled by the ease with which they opened up the French defences in the sixth minute, were much less integrated and although they earned credit for denying the French any points after half-time and for drawing level at 14–14 after trailing 4–14 at the interval, their discipline and general play were disappointing.

An early try for Edwards, scored after Mountain had made the important break on the half-way line, put Britain ahead at 4–0 and there they remained until the twenty-sixth minute when Calas, who had landed a penalty three minutes earlier when Mountain had obstructed the dangerous Baloup, dragged Loughlin with him in a powerful surge over the line.

An even better try followed from Esponella in the thirty-fourth minute after Baloup, causing enormous problems in his forays from full-back, had made an excellent long break which was then supported by Luchési. Calas added the goal points with a splendid kick from the touchline and then landed an equally fine penalty soon after Guasch had been carried from the field.

In a second half in which Britain used three substitutes, the French, physically smaller and perhaps lacking the stamina of their opponents, began to buckle under heavy, if scarcely subtle, pressure. The last fifteen minutes were particularly anxious for them and in this period tries by Divorty and Mark Wilson helped to bring Britain level.

Divorty took all the credit for his try, the loose forward following up his own high kick and then taking advantage of fumbles by both Baloup and Brencz to fall over the line. Loughlin added a simple goal.

With ten minutes remaining, it seemed that Britain might secure a fortuitous victory when Mark Wilson scored after a move that briefly looked to have been bungled. Loughlin was unable to add the goal points but it was Britain who were grateful for Calas's missed penalty and attempted drop goal. That final effort was not far wide and there could have been no serious complaints if it had brought France a win.

France Colts: Vincent Baloup (La Réole); Esponella (Pia), Calas (Châtillon), Sautrice (Pia), Amar (Avignon); Espugna (Lézignan), Pech (Limoux); Brencz (Albi, Bouscayrol (Villefranche), Rouane (Pia), Luchési (Le Pontet), Blachère (Le Pontet), Guasch (Pia)

Substitutes: Roux (Avignon) for Luchési after 68 minutes, Daffis (Villeneuve) and Chareyron (Limoux) not used

Scorers: tries – Calas, Esponella; goals – Calas (3)

Great Britain Colts: Loughlin (St Helens); Greatbatch (Castleford), Allen (St Helens), Mark Wilson (Leeds), Chapman (Castleford); Edwards (Wigan), Holden (Wigan); Mountain (Castleford), Puckering (Hull), Tomlinson (Hull), Westhead (Leigh), Gunn (Leeds), Divorty (Hull)

Substitutes: Chris Wilson (Wigan) for Gunn after 55 minutes, Mayo (Wigan) for Puckering after 63 minutes, Beazant (Leigh) for Holden after 72 minutes

Scorers: tries – Edwards, Divorty, Mark Wilson; goal – Loughlin

Referee: G. F. Lindop (England)

Attendance: 500

Albi, 16 December
France Under-21 2 Great Britain Under-21 8

It would have been nice, at the birthplace of Toulouse-Lautrec, if France and Great Britain could have shown a few artistic traits. Unfortunately this match was worse, much worse, than its forerunner at Wheldon Road. Shapeless, scrappy, at times bad-tempered, it reduced Maurice Bamford to the terse comment afterwards that, 'It was very dull and very boring . . . but it was a win on foreign soil.'

Compared with the Under-21 team that had played at Castleford, Rippon, the young Swinton full-back, who had turned professional only two months before, replaced Edwards; Gribbin, a second-division player with Whitehaven, played in the centre; Fox replaced Conway at scrum-half; and Wane, Platt and Mike Gregory came into the pack. These changes were made in an attempt to increase Bamford's knowledge of his players but the British coach must have been left wondering why youngsters who can look so impressive for their clubs can suddenly look so ordinary when picked to play at a higher level.

Again there was little inspiration from the established players. Crooks, who had been suffering from an upset stomach, felt that his legs were turning to rubber and retired before the half hour to be replaced by Round; while Schofield still appeared jaded and an uninspired afternoon ended painfully for him when he sustained a fractured arm. It was sad that, after an outstanding first season and a marvellous tour of Australia in the summer of 1984, the Hull centre should be finding it difficult to regain his form in the new season.

1   The Under-21 international against France at Castleford was a disappointing occasion, not well attended, and with a number of experienced British players below their usual form. Even so, Britain's three tries were all well taken and there was another British victory to celebrate. Here the ball flies from the grasp of Shaun Edwards, the Wigan full-back, as he is tackled during a French attack. Dannatt (Hull) is up in support with Crooks (Hull) not far behind.

Emerging with most credit from the drabness was the powerful Leeds second-row forward, Roy Powell, who had played promisingly at Castleford. He was constructive, hard working and persistent and easily the outstanding player in a dull pack. Mike Gregory also salvaged his reputation in spite of a nervous start and in spite of spending ten minutes in the sin-bin.

In the backs, Rippon made no serious error at full-back, Fox worked hard if predictably at scrum-half and Creasser tackled devotedly and showed occasional flashes of imagination. Gribbin took his try on the hour with aplomb after the most constructive British move of the afternoon, Fox and Creasser working the ball quickly right after Britain had won a scrum on the left of the French '25'.

A gruesome gash to the head ended Garcin's part in the match after only fourteen minutes. The open-side prop required lengthy treatment on the field before being helped off, clearly in distress, his legs unable to support the weight of his body, to be taken away by ambulance to hospital. That was bad luck, but the French did not help themselves with their constant lapses of discipline.

The most persistent offender was Alberola who spent one spell of ten minutes in the sin-bin and was then dismissed for good by Ronnie Campbell in the second half after the loose forward had tried to decapitate Fox as he sprinted at the French defence. That was one of the worst moments of a match in which there was a deal of ill-feeling.

As well as their bad luck and ill-discipline the French were also careless. At times they threw the ball about with imagination, but could not hold on to it at crucial moments. Their worst error came at the last when Bertheloite wasted the chance to bring France level, dropping the ball when a try seemed certain.

France's efficient tackling and covering restricted Britain to two penalties from Creasser in the first half and Gribbin's try in the second. Britain's defences, too, were sound and France's only points came from a penalty six minutes after half-time by Dumas, when Fox, somewhat harshly, was adjudged to have stolen the ball.

France Under-21: Wosniack (Villefranche); Bertheloite (Toulouse), Bret (St Estève), Lapeyre (Albi), Bessières (Albi); Berge (Le Pontet), Dumas (St Gaudens); Garcin (St Gaudens), Batello (Carcassonne), Romano (Carpentras), Cunac (Albi), Conduché (Villeneuve), Alberola (Lézignan)

Substitutes: Boulagnon (Villefranche) for Garcin after 14 minutes, Palisses (St Estève) for Batello after 61 minutes, Perez (Toulouse) not used

Scorers: goal – Dumas

Great-Britain Under-21: Rippon (Swinton); Clark (Hull KR), Schofield (Hull), Gribbin (Whitehaven), Currier (Widnes); Creasser (Leeds), Fox (Featherstone Rovers); Crooks (Hull), Groves (Salford), Wane (Wigan), Powell (Leeds), Dannatt (Hull), Gregory (Warrington)

Substitutes: Round (St Helens) for Crooks after 29 minutes, Conway (Leeds) and Tate (Hunslet) not used

Scorers: try – Gribbin; goals – Creasser (2)

Referee: R. Campbell (England)

Attendance: 2,000

Headingley, Leeds, 1 March
Great Britain 50   France 4

Great Britain's performance in the first Test at Headingley was one of the biggest, and most pleasant, surprises of the season. There had been no shortage of criticism for Maurice Bamford's side before the game started, the chief objection being that it was not the best available to him and that international caps were being given away too easily.

Bamford's players provided the best possible answer. They gave much the most fluent display a home crowd had seen since the 37–0 victory over France at the Boulevard towards the end of 1981. The discipline of the British players was impeccable and as the score began to mount the handling became increasingly assured, the support play ever more eager, the running more enthusiastic.

To win by such an overwhelming (and record) margin was to invite the accusation that Britain had had nothing to beat. But that was not the case. Indeed, for the first twenty minutes it was impossible to say which way the game would go. Macalli and Grésèque were dominant figures in midfield, both of them scurrying forward enthusiastically in an attempt to impose their patterns on the contest. Even though, by the end, the French were looking susceptible to every British attack they still retained a combative spirit, too combative for many tastes. Max Chantal in particular seemed to want to play rugby less than he wanted to knock lumps out of any opponent that came too close to him. So although the British emerged with a record haul of points, the applause of an appreciative audience ringing in their ears, and a great deal of satisfaction, there was no shortage of bruises to be nursed afterwards.

There were nine players new to Test football in the side and every man could feel gratified with his performance. Roy Dickinson was one of the older players to be winning his first cap but he clearly relished the prospect of representing his country and showed an enormous appetite for work. A less bulky man than in previous years, Dickinson displayed a surprising amount of pace and mobility.

If those were slightly unexpected qualities so too was Alan Rathbone's discipline. Rathbone has been known to fall victim to the 'red mist' that used regularly to afflict Jim Mills. But Rathbone, in spite of taking some fearful punishment, kept admirable control of himself; everyone else followed his example and if ever there was a lesson in the value of preserving the collective temper this was it.

2　Britain's remarkable victory by 50–4 against France in the first Test at Headingley was a match to savour, one of the biggest, and most pleasant, surprises of the season. On a cold, damp night both sets of forwards played with enthusiasm and genuine commitment throughout the game. Here, a pall of steam hangs in the cold air as a scrum breaks up, while the two scrum-halves, Grésèque of France, a dominant figure in the French midfield, and Fox of Britain challenge for the ball.

The willingness of Dickinson, Rathbone and Watkinson to forage and to work released the more elevated skills of Goodway, proving himself yet again a maturing forward of outstanding ability, and Divorty, whose varied passing served his side well. Fox had an excellent game at scrum-half, moving the ball with a swiftness not always previously apparent, and he was partnered by the irrepressible Hanley, who scored a try in each half, and caused the French repeated damage with his muscular runs.

Edwards's job became easier after an anxious opening and there was little criticism to be made of a three-quarter line which played its part in defence and attack, Gribbin deserving particular credit for completing successfully the

3 David Creasser, the young Leeds centre, was among those who enjoyed an outstanding game in the first Test against France at Headingley, playing with skill and imagination and kicking eight goals. Here he hands off a French defender as yet another British attack gets under way.

considerable leap from second-division to international football.

The opening twenty minutes were as competitive as could be wished with Grésèque and Macalli striving nobly to take control of the midfield but Britain released themselves from the pressure in the twenty-first minute when Creasser landed the first of his eight goals. That was followed by two tries within the space of three minutes by Hanley and Fox and the French defences, once unlocked, were to remain invitingly open.

By the interval Gill, curving round the outside edges of the French defence, had scored a third try and the British players left the field to generous applause from a crowd of 6,491, already responding to an inventive performance on a chilly, misty St David's night. They were to be treated to even more appetizing fare in the second half.

The British might have opted for an easy life after the interval. But their appetite for points was insatiable. Fox, voted the man of the match, scored his second try; Watkinson went over, juggling the ball skilfully as he did so; and Gribbin showed both finishing and distributive skills as he ran forty yards for his own try and then slipped a neat pass from which Divorty scored.

Ten minutes from time the French showed that they still possessed some spirit when the deserving Macalli who, along with the busy Grésèque, had maintained high standards from the start, scampered away for a try. But Britain had no intention of leaving the French with the last word and a thrilling break by Goodway in midfield opened up the way for Hanley to score his second try of the game.

Great Britain: Edwards (Wigan); Ledger (St Helens), Creasser (Leeds), Gribbin (Whitehaven), Gill (Wigan); Hanley (Bradford Northern), Fox (Featherstone Rovers); Dickinson (Leeds), Watkinson (Hull KR), Dannatt (Hull), Goodway (Oldham), Rathbone (Bradford Northern), Divorty (Hull)

Substitutes: Gibson (Batley) for Gill after 51 minutes, Platt (St Helens) not used

Scorers: tries – Hanley (2), Fox (2), Gill, Watkinson, Gribbin, Divorty; goals – Creasser (8), Fox

France: Pallarès (XIII Catalan); Jean (Limoux), Palisses (St Estève), Fourquet (Toulouse), Ratier (Lézignan); Perez (Toulouse), Grésèque (XIII Catalan); Chantal (Villeneuve), Macalli (Le Pontet), Meurin (Albi), Aillères (Toulouse), Guy Laforgue (XIII Catalan), Dominique Baloup (Toulouse)

Substitutes: Berge (Le Pontet) for Meurin after 56 minutes, Francis Laforgue (XIII Catalan) not used

Scorer: try – Macalli

Referee: B. Gomersall (Australia)

Attendance: 6,481

Craven Park, Hull, 2 March
Great Britain Colts 18   France Colts 10

After the high promise of their performances at Wigan the previous season and at Mazamet before Christmas, the French Colts were bitterly disappointing in losing to Britain at Craven Park, a try by Espugna eight minutes from time arriving much too late to save them. Here was an almost complete reversal of the previous season when the Colts' game at Wigan had helped to offer some compensation for the dreary Test between Great Britain and France at Leeds the previous night. Now there was little of the fluctuation of fortunes, the skill or the abandon of that game at Central Park, but instead a contest of ill-temper and stilted play, eccentrically refereed.

Seven minutes from time Espugna broke clear from a scrum won by the French in the British '25' to bring the score to 10–18 but that was one of the few moments of enterprise shown by France in a game in which they seemed to want to ape the less endearing characteristics of their seniors. It was a display which sadly forced a revision of the opinion, formed over the previous twelve months, that France possessed some very bright prospects indeed.

Britain opened imaginatively when a skilful handling move up the left wing gave Chapman the opportunity to race clear, but the score was disallowed for a forward pass, one of many bewildering decisions by M. Labadie. Thereafter, the British were increasingly drawn into the niggling, and at times highly physical, tactics adopted by the French and inevitably the game suffered.

For a time it appeared that French supremacy at this level might continue when Delarose, after collecting a loose ball in midfield, tapped the play-the-ball to himself and darted over, M. Labadie not sharing the crowd's suspicion that Delarose had knocked-on. Calas, who had earlier squandered two opportunities to put France ahead from penalties, added the goal points and France were 6 points to the good.

The craft of the Wigan scrum-half, Holden, one of the most influential figures of this contest, helped Britain back to parity only a minute before half-time. His long pass took at least two Frenchmen out of the game. Loughlin joined the line from full-back, fed Simpson with a short pass and the Bradford right winger went over forcefully in the corner.

As he did so he was fouled and Britain were awarded a penalty try. Though Loughlin was unable to land the conversion from the touchline he was still able to bring the scores level by kicking the penalty from in front of the posts. Britain, who had had to reorganize their forces after only seven minutes when they lost Westhead, were never seriously troubled again.

25

4　Ellery Hanley had a magnificent game in the first Test against France at Headingley, scoring a try in each half and causing the French repeated damage with his muscular runs. Here he catches a 'bomb' with secure hands but with the French full-back, Pallarès, waiting to tackle.

Loughlin put them ahead with a penalty in the forty-sixth minute and soon afterwards Britain produced their best move of the afternoon, Ford, Mayo, Chris Wilson, Mark Wilson and Chapman combining to make a deserved try for Harcombe, Westhead's replacement, whose assurance had burgeoned after a nervous beginning.

Medley, who had a good overall match and an especially fine second half, was then heavily involved in Britain's third try in the fifty-first minute, scored by Allen and converted by Loughlin. From 18–6 there was no way back for the French, who, too late, began to throw the ball about in a way which, if sustained, would probably have brought them much greater reward than Espugna's late try.

Great Britain Colts: Loughlin (St Helens); Simpson (Bradford Northern), Allen (St Helens), Mark Wilson (Leeds), Chapman (Castleford); Ford (Wigan), Holden (Wigan); Wood (Hunslet), Hughes (Leigh), Mayo (Wigan), Medley (Leeds), Chris Wilson (Wigan), Westhead (Leigh)

Substitutes: Harcombe (Doncaster) for Westhead after 7 minutes, Mountain (Castleford) for Wood at half-time, Beazant (Leigh) for Simpson after 69 minutes

Scorers: tries – Simpson, Harcombe, Allen; goals – Loughlin (3)

France Colts: Vincent Baloup (La Réole); Esponella (Pia), Delarose (Carcassonne), Sautrice (Pia), Kidrazinski (Villeneuve); Calas (Châtillon), Espugna (Lézignan); Brencz (Albi), Bouscayrol (Villefranche), Rouane (Pia), Blachère (Le Pontet), Charayron (Limoux), Luchési (Le Pontet)

Substitutes: Scarabbini (Villeneuve) for Kidrazinski after 55 minutes, Pech (Limoux) for Delarose after 76 minutes, Roux (Entraigues) for Charayron after 76 minutes

Scorers: tries – Delarose, Espugna; goal – Calas

Referee: C. Labadie (France)

Attendance: 500

Stade Gilbert Brutus, Perpignan, 17 March
France 24   Great Britain 16

The return Test at Perpignan saw a welcome revival of French rugby. France had been beaten in the five previous Tests by Britain; they had a long string of Under-24 defeats stretching behind them, and only a couple of successes in Colts games to relieve the depression. So their unconfined delight at the end of this game was justified and understandable.

Bamford, pursuing his policy of using as many players in his squad as possible, made changes from Leeds and without question the side was weakened. Then, on the morning of the match, Andy Goodway, Britain's captain and best forward, had to withdraw suffering from influenza. That brought in Dannatt with Hanley taking over the captaincy.

Other changes were made at full-back where the young Chris Johnson, no doubt grateful for once to escape from his struggling club side, Leigh, replaced Edwards; in the centre Foy came in for Gribbin. On the wings Clark and Phil Ford took over from Ledger and Gill while Wane and Kiss helped to form a new front row with Dickinson.

The French had made changes too, for the better as it transpired. It was thought that Wosniack, such an impressive young full-back the previous season, would replace Pallarès and that Solal, well known to British supporters through his time spent at Hull, would come in on the right wing, but both, again, were injured.

However, France did opt for change in the three-quarters with Ratier switching to the right wing and Couston coming in on the left; at stand-off Perez made way for Francis Laforgue; Titeux replaced Meurin at blind-side prop. Montgaillard and Verdes came into the second row and Guy Laforgue moved to loose forward instead of Dominique Baloup.

At the back of many British minds was the memory of Marseilles in 1981. Defeat there had followed crushing success at the Boulevard, where Gill and Drummond had scored five tries between them, throwing into confusion the plans of the British management pair of Johnny Whiteley and Colin Hutton. The caution was justified because the French, never a predictable nation, again turned the tables spectacularly.

By the end the French were looking much less secure than at half-time. They failed to score a point in the second half and over the final ten minutes looked tired to the point of exhaustion. But their win was thoroughly deserved, based as it was on a first half in which they had displayed many of their more endearing qualities.

5　The second Test against France, at Perpignan, saw a welcome revival of French rugby. France won a tough but absorbing contest by 24–16 and looked the more progressive side. Here Francis Laforgue, the French stand-off, comes across in an attempt to intercept Andy Dannatt (Hull) in full flight, while Couston, the French left wing, acts as cover.

Their opening try was memorable, a breathtaking score, that brought the crowd to a rare pitch of excitement. Montgaillard began the movement by boring a hole clean through the British first line of defence. First Verdes took up the running and then Grésèque, who threw out a ball that at best could be described as hopeful. But racing up at speed was the French left centre, Palisses, who gathered it beautifully and then fed Couston for the left winger to score the first of his three tries.

Few sides would have had an answer to that score and not surprisingly it inspired the French. The match developed into a tough but absorbing contest but with the French looking the more progressive side. Phil Ford, who made a promising first appearance on the left wing, helped to bring the scores level only six minutes after France's opening try, but then two lapses helped to take the French almost out of reach.

First, Hanley's pass was intercepted by Fourquet. He ran sixty yards before he was hauled down by Ford but the British defence was in so much disarray that France were able to score on the next tackle as the ball was worked right and Couston, now appearing on his opposite wing, went over in the corner. No sooner had Britain had time to contemplate that blunder than a pass by Divorty, deep in French territory, was intercepted by Couston.

Creasser chased him but could not catch him; Johnson seemed to have jockeyed himself into a position from which he looked ready to launch a try-saving tackle but his judgement was faulty and when he did begin to close in it was too late. Couston went round him and raced clear to the line. Just before half-time France scored again. The ever-dangerous Montgaillard resisted Ford's attempt to haul him down and his break brought a try for Fourquet. Pallarès, looking a much more secure full-back than at Leeds, helped the French cause considerably by landing four goals.

The arrears of 18 points were too great for Britain to overhaul but they did enjoy much better fortune in the second half, scoring two tries and a goal while freezing the French score at 24 points. Hanley was seen at his best soon after the interval when he made a long foray into French territory, finally being halted only a few yards from the French line. The damage had been done, however, and Foy, from acting half-back, was able to dart over the line.

Fox had made way for Harkin at the interval and the Hull KR scrum-half helped to tighten Britain's play in midfield. He provided a much greater sense of urgency and much needed drive, and when Ford, side-stepping Guy Laforgue on his way to the line, scored his second good try it seemed that Britain might yet salvage something. Tempers were starting to fray, with Foy, Chantal and Guy Laforgue spending ten minutes in the sin-bin, and the French were also tiring rapidly ... but not so rapidly that they were going to let this famous victory slip.

France: Pallarès (XIII Catalan); Ratier (Lézignan), Fourquet (Toulouse), Palisses (St Estève), Couston (Carpentras); Francis Laforgue (XIII Catalan), Grésèque (XIII Catalan); Chantal (Villeneuve), Macalli (Le Pontet), Titeux (Le Pontet), Montgaillard (XIII Catalan), Verdes (Villeneuve), Guy Laforgue (XIII Catalan)

Substitutes: Mendes (Limoux) for Palisses after 36 minutes, Bernabé (Le Pontet) for Mendes after 68 minutes

Scorers: tries – Couston (3), Fourquet; goals – Pallarès (4)

Great Britain: Johnson (Leigh); Clark (Hull KR), Creasser (Leeds), Foy (Oldham), Ford (Wigan); Hanley (Bradford Northern), Fox (Featherstone Rovers); Dickinson (Leeds), Kiss (Wigan), Wane (Wigan), Dannatt (Hull), Rathbone (Bradford Northern), Divorty (Hull)

Substitutes: Harkin (Hull KR) for Fox at half-time, Powell (Leeds) for Dickinson after 56 minutes

Scorers: tries – Ford (2), Foy; goals – Creasser, Divorty

Referee: B. Gomersall (Australia)

Attendance: 5,500

Paul Fitzpatrick

2

THE JOHN PLAYER SPECIAL TROPHY, THE PHILIPS VIDEO YORKSHIRE CUP AND THE BURTONWOOD BREWERY LANCASHIRE CUP

THE JOHN PLAYER SPECIAL TROPHY

One of the more surprising features of Rugby League in recent years had been the fact that Hull Kingston Rovers, who have been such a force in the game, had never won the John Player Trophy. It was an omission they put right on an icy January day in 1985. Like Hull in the final of the Yorkshire Cup three months earlier, Rovers rejoiced in the fact that victory in the final had been achieved over their great rivals from across the city. Both sides had suffered alarms on their way to the final: Hull had trailed by no less than 0–14 in the first round at Fulham and Rovers were 0–8 down to Halifax in the semi-final. However, Rovers not only scored three tries in beating Hull in the final but did not concede a point. Their 12–0 victory was seen by a record crowd for the competition of 25,326, who paid receipts of £69,555 at Boothferry Park. Revenge had a splendid taste.

Because of the awkward number of professional clubs taking part in the competition it was decided to accommodate two amateur teams in the preliminary round and the National Trophy finalists of the previous season were admitted – Myson's from Hull and the Bradford side, Dudley Hill. Myson's met Dewsbury at the Boulevard on a dreadful Friday night and emerged with great credit. They restricted the professionals to just one try, scored by the New Zealand centre, Chris Mita, and went down by only 2–8.

Dudley Hill were drawn at Keighley, virtually a local derby fixture, and there was the teasing possibility, if they won, of visiting St Helens, now with the Australian star Mal Meninga in the side, for the first round draw had already been made. Though Dudley Hill had a man sent off in the first half, they gave a splendid account of themselves before being beaten 10–24.

There was only one preliminary round surprise, newcomers Sheffield Eagles beating Wakefield Trinity 17–6, much to the satisfaction of their player-manager Gary Hetherington. Victory over one of his old clubs meant a visit to Leeds in the next round; but there the fairy story ended. Leeds scored ten tries in a 50–2 win.

It was a round of high scoring. Topping the list were Whitehaven, whose Great Britain Under-21 centre, Vince Gribbin, grabbed six tries, a club and competition record, in the 64–0 hiding of luckless Doncaster. There were ten tries for St Helens, Barry Ledger scoring three, and Sean Day adding ten goals in the 60–8 win over Keighley. Wigan, after being held for some time, cut loose with five tries in eighteen minutes in the second half to register a 50–6 win over Huddersfield. Bridgend switched their tie against Castleford to Wheldon Road. A crowd of 1,795 was considerably better than would have turned up at Coychurch Road, but there was little other cause for Welsh satisfaction as they went down 4–42.

Hull had suffered shocks at Fulham before and seemed to be on their way to another as the Londoners led 14–0 just before the interval. But the wizardry of scrum-half Peter Sterling brought a try for Lee Crooks and Hull scored 28 points in eleven minutes either side of half-time to run out 36–14 winners.

Dewsbury raised a few eyebrows with a 14–8 home win over Salford, and Halifax gave warning of things to come with an impressive 17–5 success at Warrington. A last-minute try by winger Dave Dyas gave Bramley a sketchy win over Blackpool Borough, who had dominated for long periods, and Rochdale Hornets did well to pip Mansfield 10–8, three goals by Billy Platt proving crucial.

Widnes were given a fright before winning 22–12 at Workington, Featherstone Rovers had to work hard to edge out Barrow, and there were victories for Bradford Northern over Swinton, and for Oldham at York. Enthusiastic Runcorn Highfield's spirits soared as Peter Wood landed four goals and two drop goals in an 18–5 triumph over Batley, and Hull KR had already issued a warning to all opponents with a 32–5 televised victory over Leigh.

The big attractions in the second round were Leeds at home to Wigan,

33

Bradford Northern at home to St Helens, and Hull with a match against Oldham. All three proved tremendous contests. A Saturday crowd of 9,248 revelled in a marvellous cut-and-thrust affair at Leeds. Terry Webb burrowed over to put Leeds ahead and David Creasser added the goal. But Wigan struck back with a superb solo try by Australian winger John Ferguson, who was proving a big favourite at Central Park. Only two points separated the sides until the Leeds half-back, John Holmes, ghosted his way up the wing, drew the cover and timed his inside pass perfectly for the Australian centre, Tony Currie, to score from forty-five yards out. Even then Leeds had to survive a mighty Wigan onslaught before going through.

A crowd of 9,419 saw high drama and controversy at Odsal as St Helens had their substitute Roy Haggerty sent off before the interval in their match against Bradford Northern. Bradford's winger, David Smith, had scored a surprise try, chasing a kick ahead without much hope but diving for the touchdown when the ball seemed to stop on the sloping corner at Odsal. St Helens rallied superbly, although Northern bitterly contested a try by Ledger in the second half, before a late Steve Parrish penalty goal brought a 12–12 draw. The replay attracted over 10,000 to Knowsley Road and again St Helens had a man sent off in the first half, this time Paul Round. But Neil Holding was in superb form and grabbed two tries to enable St Helens to go through by 24–10.

Inevitably, the biggest crowd of the round was at the Boulevard, where 11,500 saw Hull beat Oldham 26–14. Andy Goodway was in storming form and scored two tries for Oldham but Hull had the greater all-round skill, with Sterling and fellow Australian John Muggleton among their five try-scorers.

Halifax caused a sensation by sacking their popular coach Colin Dixon just before the home tie with Castleford, replacing him with the experienced Australian Chris Anderson who had just joined the club from Hull KR. It was not a popular move among the Thrum Hall supporters, and with a large number of Australians already at the club it caused unrest among the English players, who felt they were being pushed out. When Halifax trailed 8–16 to Castleford, things looked grim. However, splendidly led by scrum-half Michael Hagan, Halifax battled back. Even then Castleford seemed to have settled things when a penalty goal nudged them 18–14 ahead with three minutes left. But they committed the amazing mistake of trying to throw the ball around in their own '25' and lost possession. Tony Anderson swerved his way over and Malcolm Agar's goal gave Halifax a 20–18 win. Chris Anderson remarked, 'We got out of gaol.' The comments of opposing coach Malcolm Reilly are not recorded but can be imagined.

Widnes comfortably beat Featherstone, Hull KR defeated Rochdale, and Dewsbury maintained progress with a bright first-half showing to beat

Runcorn. Bramley caused a real upset by hammering Whitehaven 33–5.

The competition's tendency to provide talking points was maintained in the third round, when Halifax visited St Helens in a televised fixture. St Helens were in tremendous form after thirteen games without defeat, while Halifax, under much criticism for taking on so many Australian players, still had a case to prove. They provided a devastating reply. Full-back Mario Cerchione, one of only four Englishmen in the team, raised question marks about the Saints' defence by forcing his way over for the first try. Halifax played up to the lead, tackling with rare fervour to knock the home team out of their stride. Had Agar not failed with seven of his eight shots at goal in the first half, Halifax would have been out of sight by the interval, instead of only 6–0 ahead. It became 8–0 before Day was awarded an obstruction try and added the goal to make it 8–6 and set the scene for a St Helens revival. It did not materialize. St Helens were penalized near their own posts and fatally turned their backs, clearly expecting a shot at goal. Chris Anderson spotted the lapse and took a quick tap to send Agar over at the corner. The latter rubbed in the salt by adding the touchline goal and Halifax held on for a tremendous 14–8 triumph.

That upset dominated the third round, although Hull KR had to hold off a determined Widnes challenge at Craven Park. Rovers looked to their strong pack to grind Widnes into submission but a snap try by David Lyon and the goal by Mick Burke gave Widnes a 6–2 interval lead. Second-row forward Andrew Kelly had a try disallowed in the first half but continued to give the visiting defence many problems. However, when the break came it was a surprise. Rovers won a heel against the head and Paul Harkin nipped round the blindside to find he had a clear fifteen-yard run to the line. George Fairbairn added the goal and Rovers never looked back. Gavin Miller, rapidly finding his feet at loose forward for Rovers, combined with Kelly for Fairbairn to stretch the home lead, and he rounded things off with a penalty.

Dewsbury's third-round appearance gave them a welcome lift. Strong work by Mita and non-stop tackling by the Australian Tony Murphy were important elements in a basically youthful side. The visit of Hull attracted 7,200 to Crown Flatt, a ground where the season's average at that point was less than 1,000. They saw a rousing performance by Dewsbury, who trailed only 8–10 at the interval before first division quality emerged and Hull scored five tries to one for a 22–8 success.

Bramley, the other second division representatives in the third round, were also far from disgraced against neighbours Leeds at Headingley. Leeds won 28–14 but all three Bramley tries by Hayden Kelly, Steve Carroll and Dave Dyas were of a sufficiently high quality to make nonsense of their lowly league position.

The semi-final draw, Hull KR v Halifax and Hull v Leeds, raised the exciting

6　The final of the John Player Special Trophy was played in arctic conditions at Boothferry Park, Hull KR beating Hull 12–0. Here Gary Prohm, Rovers' outstanding New Zealand centre, scores their first try in a flurry of snow.

prospect of an all-Humberside final. The timing of the matches was to prove important and controversial. Hull KR were due to meet Halifax at Headingley on 29 December and Rovers promptly postponed their Boxing Day league visit to Hunslet, as was their right. Halifax were in a quandary. The great win at St Helens had whipped up interest and they had an attractive Boxing Day fixture at home to Bradford Northern. Should they postpone the Northern game and rest for the semi-final, only three days later, or cash in on the enthusiasm their success at St Helens had generated?

After considerable thought Halifax elected to play on Boxing Day. Reward came with a 24–8 victory for two important league points before a crowd of 6,451, easily their best of the season to date. The price was paid later.

Halifax produced a stunning first-half display in the semi-final to shake Hull

KR to the roots. They ran with spirit and enterprise and tackled non-stop. A tremendous break by Chris Anderson created a good try for Paul Langmack and the goal by Agar put Halifax 6–0 ahead at the interval and it could easily have been more. A penalty goal by Agar soon after the resumption made it 8–0 and another shock was on the cards. Rovers, though, are seasoned to this type of test. Their pack, with David Watkinson, Miller and Mark Broadhurst in fine form, took charge and Paul Harkin began to dictate play, making superb use of the touchline. Yet it took a Halifax error to change the pattern as Garry Clark ran fifty yards to turn defence into attack. The ball was moved swiftly to Gary Prohm who swept over for a good try and Fairbairn added the goal. The transformation was dramatic. Halifax suddenly looked a spent force and weariness showed in the way their cover failed to nail Clark, who stylishly took half a chance to score a top-class winger's try at the corner to put Rovers ahead. Another neatly worked move enabled Mike Smith to score unopposed and send Rovers to the final. Inevitably Halifax blamed the Boxing Day game for their fade-out, while acknowledging the quality of the Rovers play in the last half-hour.

Hull's game with Leeds was on 5 January at Boothferry Park. Hull had played the previous Sunday and had no New Year fixture. Leeds were due to entertain Leigh on New Year's Day and had their Australian Test star Eric Grothe making his debut. There was therefore no question of postponing the Leigh match though it was only four days before the semi-final. Leeds won comfortably by 38–4 and Grothe scored three sensational tries. But again there was a penalty to pay. The Leeds front three, Roy Dickinson, David Ward and Gavin Jones, were injured in the match and ruled out of the semi-final.

The three players were badly missed. The Hull pack dominated the match throughout and the whole team gave a magnificent display to destroy Leeds. Steve Norton organized the pack in great style and scrum-half Peter Sterling again emphasized his class with an outstanding display. He completed a notable double for scrum-halves by following Harkin in taking the man of the match award. There was also a bonus for Hull in a good display by Paul Prendiville, who had collected a winner's medal on the wing with Leeds the previous season. Prendiville was in his old position of full-back in the absence of Gary Kemble and played with complete confidence. He missed with an early shot at goal from Fred Ah Kuoi's well-taken try but from that point did not put a hand or foot wrong. Although sharp play by Currie enabled Creasser to level matters midway through the first half, Leeds never looked like winning. Hull led 6–4 at the interval and second-half tries from Wayne Proctor, a splendid forty-yard effort, and James Leuluai enabled Hull to coast home 18–6.

So the stage was set for another major confrontation of the two Humberside teams and the natural venue was again Boothferry Park.

John Player Special Trophy Final
Boothferry Park, Hull, 26 January
Hull KR 12   Hull 0

While Rovers were trying to win the Trophy for the first time, Hull still had fond memories of their triumph in 1982, when they beat their neighbours in the final at Headingley. The closeness of the Rugby League fraternity on Humberside was emphasized once again on the morning of the match when supporters from both clubs worked with groundstaff to help free the pitch of its covering of snow and ice.

Rovers were without Andy Kelly, which meant a relatively rare appearance for Phil Hogan, while Hull, crucially, were without Norton and the Australian second-row forward John Muggleton. There was another lively opening with both sides soon moving the ball around. Hull made the first clean break as Paul Rose slipped out a neat pass to send Ah Kuoi racing up the left flank. He almost made it to the corner and when challenged threw a desperate and rather wayward pass inside which Leuluai, hampered by defenders, was unable to take.

Rose revived memories of his dismissal in the Yorkshire Cup final when he became embroiled with the Rovers' forwards and one tussle with Miller earned him a stern warning. From that penalty award Rovers struck hard. Miller was involved in the smart build-up, which sent Ian Robinson racing diagonally for the left corner. His pass to the wing was knocked down but bounced favourably for Gary Prohm to gather and dive over for the first try after fourteen minutes. Rovers played up to their lead, keeping the Boulevard defence at full stretch, and five minutes later they scored again. Miller was prominent once more as his pass gave Hogan space. He made full use of it, shaking off a tackle to break clear and show fine pace to score near the corner. Rovers now led 8–0 and their only worry at this stage was the memory of the county final when they had held a similar lead. And, as before, Fairbairn had not landed a goal. But Hull were not looking as sharp and they suffered a further set-back when they lost Kemble with concussion, Garry Schofield taking his place.

Hull had plenty of scrum possession, and the penalty count favoured them, but they failed to crack a Rovers defence in which Watkinson, Miller and Broadhurst were outstanding. Harkin varied his tactics with great skill and his tactical kicking constantly drove Hull back.

In the second half Hull had much more of the play but clearly missed the craft

7 Gavin Miller, the Australian loose forward, made a tremendous impact in his first season for Hull KR. Here he avoids the despairing tackle of Hull's loose forward, Gary Divorty, in the John Player Special Trophy final. In support is the reliable Mark Broadhurst.

of Norton and the supporting ability of Muggleton. Clean breaks were rare. When one came, Hull's best of the match, it fell to Andy Dannatt, who had just taken the field as substitute for Phil Edmonds. Dannatt had only Fairbairn to beat and men in support but fatally delayed his pass and the Rovers' full-back made a crunching smother tackle. It was Hull's last chance. Rovers drove them back and Hogan again showed pace and neat footwork to create space in the opposing '25' before lobbing a finely-judged pass for Clark to score the third try and complete a 12–0 win. Harkin again took the man of the match award and earned glowing praise for his display from his opposite number, Sterling.

Hull KR: Fairbairn; Clark, Robinson, Prohm, Laws; Mike Smith, Harkin; Broadhurst, Watkinson, Ema, Burton, Hogan, Miller

Substitutes: Lydiat and Casey not used

Scorers: tries – Prohm, Hogan, Clark

Hull: Kemble; Evans, Ah Kuoi, Leuluai, O'Hara; Topliss, Sterling; Edmonds, Patrick, Rose, Crooks, Proctor, Divorty

Substitutes: Schofield for Kemble after 21 minutes, Dannatt for Edmonds after 62 minutes

Referee: S. Wall (Leigh)

Attendance: 25,326

Trevor Watson

THE PHILIPS VIDEO YORKSHIRE CUP

It was easy to understand Hull's delight after winning the Philips Video Yorkshire Cup for a record-equalling third successive time. They not only became the second club to do so, joining Huddersfield, who had performed the feat more than sixty years before, but their triumph was achieved after a remarkable fight-back against their old Humberside rivals in a spectacular and absorbing game.

Hull's performance was astonishing, coming back from a seemingly hopeless score of 0–12 to run riot and win 29–12. It was all the more praiseworthy for Hull had been out of touch and not playing particularly well by their own high standards. With the exception of their resounding semi-final success over Leeds, they had seemed uncertain in too many of their matches. Indeed, they had raised eyebrows even before the first round of the competition when coach Arthur Bunting had suspended four of his players for having a drink before training.

Thus, in the first round, Gary Kemble, Paul Prendiville, Lee Crooks and Steve Norton were all unavailable for the home tie with Halifax. It says much for the professionalism of the club that there were no complaints from the men involved. They simply got on with the job of regaining their places. Bunting's act was a brave one. Had Hull lost to Halifax he would doubtless have found himself with few supporters. It wasn't the first time he had backed his judgement with action. There was, for example, the selection of an unknown

40

8 No success this time for Hull KR's fast developing young prop, 'Zook' Ema, as he is brought to earth in a flying tackle by Hull's Lee Crooks in the Yorkshire Cup final.

youngster, Garry Schofield, in the previous year's final in preference to experienced internationals. Bunting was to spring another surprise before the final when he gave the team captaincy to Lee Crooks. On each occasion fortune favoured the brave and decisive. In any event, after a few early anxious moments Hull beat Halifax 30–10 with Steve Evans scoring two tries. The show was on the road again.

In other ties, Bradford Northern's Ellery Hanley produced a devastating performance against Wakefield Trinity. He had warmed up in mid-week with a hat-trick of tries in the league win over Featherstone Rovers at Odsal. He went one better at Belle Vue and added two goals as Northern made Trinity supporters long for past glories with a crowning 30–0 win. With Castleford and Featherstone Rovers also drawn at home, Trinity had experimented with a Saturday fixture, but the attendance of 2,303 for an attractive tie was not a success.

Castleford entertained Leeds, who were still waiting for the majority of their Australians to arrive and had only Terry Webb on duty. They also lacked John Holmes, injured in an accident at work. Leeds won rather more convincingly than the 16–14 score suggested, Castleford's last 6 points coming in the dying seconds.

Featherstone Rovers, so often responsible for cup upsets over the years were perilously close to being on the receiving end when they trailed at home 12–17 in the last two minutes to a spirited Batley side. However, Rovers preserved their dignity with a try by Alan Dakin and the reliable Steve Quinn added the goal to leave Batley convinced there is no justice in life.

Prop Peter Clayton scored the only try as Bramley won a dour game 12–4 at Dewsbury and Huddersfield edged through 9–6 at home to Keighley. Hull KR demolished luckless Doncaster 48–4, the talking point being a crowd of 1,889 at Tatters Field, more used to a sprinkling of 250. York beat Hunslet for the second successive season, stand-off Graham Steadman scoring two dazzling tries and landing four goals in a 20–16 win.

The outstanding tie of the second round was Bradford Northern against Leeds at the strange-looking Odsal Stadium, which had lost its main stand as part of a massive improvement scheme. The crowd of 7,550 saw a tense battle. Leeds sprang a surprise by including Holmes for his first game of the season. He promptly made his mark, creating an early try for Gary Moorby, giving Leeds a 9–4 advantage at the interval. The second half was little more than a siege of the Leeds line. Northern tried forward rushes, high kicks, short kicks, Hanley's probes and Alan Rathbone's strong breaks. There were some desperate moments but Leeds survived, and in one of their rare attacks David Ward landed a drop-goal to make the score 10–4.

The other ties went very much according to expectations. Hull travelled to York and ran away with things in the last quarter to win 38–8, with Schofield scoring two tries and landing seven goals. Hull KR experienced some difficulty against gritty Huddersfield at Craven Park. The visitors were finally cracked by Gary Prohm's fiftieth try for Rovers as they won 18–2. Consolation for Huddersfield lay in the fact that they were the first team to hold Rovers to less than 30 points during the season. Bramley tackled hard but went down 2–18 to Featherstone Rovers and prospects of an all-Humberside final loomed large when the Hull pair were kept apart in the semi-final draw, much to the relief of the Yorkshire treasurer.

The first responsibility lay with Hull, who entertained Leeds, a side they had beaten in their last seven meetings. There was an expectant crowd of 10,775 at the Boulevard despite the fact that Hull had not been playing particularly well and had lost three of their first five league matches. The Headingley side had their newly-arrived Australian Test forward Wally Fullerton-Smith making his debut along with fellow Australian Steve Bleakley, and the two must have wondered what had hit them as Hull settled into what had become their usual high-speed form against Leeds.

From the moment Schofield swooped on a Leeds error over their line when they failed to cover his kick ahead, Hull's win was never in doubt. They played quality rugby, with Fred Ah Kuoi in sparkling form at scrum-half. Scoring honours went to Schofield with three more tries and three goals to add to his growing tally against Leeds. Two of his touchdowns were magnificent. For one, a Webb kick was taken deep in his own '25' by Gary Kemble and he swept past the Leeds defence to send James Leuluai free up the touchline. Schofield was in support to crown a glorious move, and soon after he intercepted and ran eighty yards to complete his hat-trick.

Hull KR were at Featherstone Rovers twenty-four hours later in the second semi-final. They endured some early anxious moments against a lively attack and David Hobbs was held only inches short. But once Hull KR clicked into gear, the issue was never really in doubt. They scored four tries in a 22–2 success and had other tries disallowed. Gary Prohm started things moving after Ian Robinson's good break and there were other touchdowns from David Laws, David Hall and Garry Clark. Perhaps the best came from Clark, for it stemmed from marvellous combined work by the Hull KR front three as 'Zook' Ema, Mark Broadhurst and David Watkinson linked to send the winger clear. The stage was set for yet another Humberside spectacular and this time in their own backyard at Boothferry Park.

The Yorkshire Cup Final
Boothferry Park, Hull, 27 October
Hull 29   Hull KR 12

It was the third all-Hull county final. Rovers had won the previous two, by 2–0 in 1920 and 8–7 in 1967, when Roger Millward, now their coach, had scored one of the tries. A significant boost for Hull was that their brilliant Australian scrum-half, Peter Sterling, had rejoined them. He had arrived unaware that his side had reached the final but was to relish the occasion. Rovers, on the other hand, had the encouragement of having fought back from 2–16 down to win 27–16 in the league game between the sides at Craven Park a fortnight earlier.

Both teams suffered set-backs in the weekend prior to the final. Rovers lost

9   Lee Crooks holds aloft the Yorkshire Cup after a fighting revival by Hull had brought them victory by 29–12, Crooks himself scoring a try.

their unbeaten record at home to Wigan, while Hull lost an incredible game at Leigh. That match had served one important purpose, however, for it had enabled Sterling to gain vital match practice. Rovers were without Gordon Smith, injured in the semi-final win at Featherstone, but had a sound replacement in Paul Harkin. Some regular supporters of both clubs were upset that the game was played on a Saturday in spite of the fact that the BBC were not showing the match 'live'. Yet fans rallied round and the attendance of 24,953 was the best for a Yorkshire final for twenty-six years and receipts of £68,639 easily a record.

Rovers began like a whirlwind, throwing the ball around with confidence to score three tries in the first half-hour and lead 12–0. Robinson raced in for the first after nine minutes and the surprise was that it took Rovers a further sixteen minutes before scoring again, when George Fairbairn forced his way over. Hall, whose handling skills had done much to keep his side ticking over, collected the third, and it seemed immaterial that Rovers had not landed a goal. Even during that spell of Rovers superiority, however, there had been signs that Hull could be dangerous. Wayne Proctor missed one chance when he dropped Steve Norton's pass when well placed, and Norton, Sterling and Phil Edmonds made it clear they did not regard the issue as settled.

A Schofield penalty put Hull on the scoreboard and just before the interval they got the try they were seeking when Sterling's shrewd kick enabled Crooks to plunge over. Schofield's goal made it only 12–8 to Rovers at half-time and the pressure was on.

There was a sensation within two minutes of the resumption as Gary Kemble gathered a Rovers drop-out, sliced through the first line of defence, and had the pace to beat the cover for a brilliant try. Schofield's fine goal pushed Hull 14–12 ahead and Sterling now took charge. He organized the flowing Hull attacks and his tactical kicking kept unhappy Rovers on tenterhooks. Schofield hoisted a drop-goal to stretch Hull's lead and Kemble scored his second splendid try to give his side breathing space at 19–12.

It was scarcely needed. Brilliant combined play enabled Norton to walk over the fourth try, Schofield added the goal and Hull rounded things off when Evans intercepted to gallop ninety yards for the last try. The match still had a bizarre finale when Hull's substitute, Paul Rose, was sent off for an attempted high tackle less than two minutes after taking the field. Sterling took his first man of the match award and clearly he had more to follow.

Hull: Kemble; Leuluai, Schofield, Evans, O'Hara; Ah Kuoi, Sterling; Edmonds, Patrick, Crooks, Norton, Proctor, Divorty

Substitutes: Rose for Divorty after 73 minutes, Topliss not used

Scorers: tries – Kemble (2), Crooks, Norton, Evans; goals – Schofield (4); drop goal – Schofield

Hull KR: Fairbairn; Clark, Robinson, Prohm, Laws; Mike Smith, Harkin; Broadhurst, Watkinson, Ema, Burton, Kelly, Hall

Substitutes: Hartley for Ema after 54 minutes, Rudd for Harkin after 79 minutes

Scorers: tries – Robinson, Fairbairn, Hall

Referee: G. F. Lindop (Wakefield)

Attendance: 24,953

Trevor Watson

THE BURTONWOOD BREWERY LANCASHIRE CUP

After Barrow's dramatic run and eventual triumph over Widnes the previous year, the 1984 Burtonwood Brewery Lancashire Cup competition made much statelier progress. But it was no less exciting or memorable for that.

The biggest shock came in the first round and, oddly enough, Oldham were the unhappy victims. In 1983 they had failed against second-division Swinton in the second round at Station Road. This time they left their supporters distressed by going out to another second-division club, Blackpool Borough, even more shamefully on their home ground at Watersheddings. Borough won 32–26 and thoroughly deserved their taste of glory. The reliable Norman Turley kicked six goals, but the man who made his mark most forcibly was prop Hugh Waddell, whose two tries and hard running did so much to upset Oldham.

Manager Frank Myler, as distressed as any of Oldham's supporters, praised Borough, but was sharply critical of his team. 'We were 14 points up and sat back,' he complained. 'In cup ties this sometimes happens. Hopefully, it has been a lesson well learned. Blackpool played well and all credit to them. They took advantage of us. We started panicking and giving silly passes.' Myler added world-wearily, 'I've seen it all before.' As indeed he had – at Swinton a year earlier.

Barrow, the holders, had a comfortable 38–4 win over Carlisle but Widnes flopped 8–28 against Wigan at Central Park. It was a marvellous match for Graeme West, Wigan's New Zealand captain; he scored two tries and inspired his packmates. There were no upsets – Oldham apart – but, significantly, St Helens ran up 58 points to Runcorn's 14. Even more significantly, perhaps, Mal Meninga, the Australian Test centre, had yet to arrive at Knowsley Road to make one of the greatest impacts of the season. Quite an impression was created by a comparatively unknown winger, Sean Day, who kicked nine goals for St Helens, a sharp hint of good things to come.

There were some close ties: Salford scraped home 19–14 against Whitehaven; Fulham were forced to surrender home advantage because their new ground at Crystal Palace was not available, yet failed by only 18–25 at Swinton; Leigh had to work hard to beat Warrington; while Rochdale Hornets exposed Workington's many weaknesses by winning 11–0 at Derwent Park.

Blackpool Borough's touch of triumph proved brief for they were beaten 6–15 by Salford at the Willows in the second round in a tie more notable for effort than class. Borough looked so ordinary that how they managed to beat Oldham remained one of the mysteries of the season. The other ties followed predictable courses. Of the fancied teams, Leigh faced stubborn resistance before winning 22–10 away to Rochdale Hornets.

Swinton, trailing 0–10 at half-time, never offered serious opposition to Wigan and lost 6–32. The tie presented a classic example of the gap between the first and second divisions; Wigan had the speed and penetration while Swinton could only give courage and effort. John Ferguson, the Australian on Wigan's right wing, confirmed his outstanding form with two tries while loose forward John Pendlebury kicked six goals out of eight attempts. St Helens travelled to Barrow and were scarcely extended in winning 26–10. Even better news for Saints was that Meninga and the Brisbane full-back Phil Vievers were on their way.

By the time the semi-final draw was made the finalists were as good as decided – St Helens and Wigan. Saints crushed Leigh 38–10 at Knowsley Road and Meninga's awesome power was displayed in the two tries he scored. Vievers, too, looked sharp and took his try stylishly. Meninga also kicked two goals, but was to hand over this chore to Day's steady boot.

It was not such an easy ride for Wigan against Salford at the Willows. Salford lifted their game and led 8–2 at half-time through a try by the New Zealand full-back Roby Muller and two goals by centre David Twist to a penalty by full-back Shaun Edwards. Salford, without injured regulars Mick McTigue, Denis Boyd and Stewart Williams, dominated the first half, and the tackling of Eric Prescott and Colin Meachin frustrated all Wigan's attempts to open out the game.

Wigan did not even the score until the forty-fourth minute, when centre David Stephenson, a Salford old boy, scored and Colin Whitfield, another old Salfordian, added the goal. It was only in the last ten minutes that Wigan's extra class and speed outflanked a tenacious Salford defence. Stephenson scored a second try, the Australian Mark Cannon, a commanding stand-off in the second half, scored another and Whitfield kicked one goal and dropped another four minutes from time.

The stage was not quite set for the final: the Lancashire county committee, acting somewhat hastily, had already selected Warrington's Wilderspool ground as the venue. St Helens and Wigan, confident of massive support, protested that Wilderspool's 16,000 capacity would prevent thousands of their followers from seeing the match. They made their point successfully and it was agreed to play the match at Wigan. So for the first time the final was not staged on a neutral ground and, also for the first time, it was played on a Sunday. The usual Saturday date was discarded because the BBC in its infinite wisdom had decided only to film highlights for later screening in a magazine programme.

The historians also pointed out that St Helens and Wigan had met only once before in the final in the seventy-nine years of the competition. Some also saw an omen in the result on that other occasion – a 16–8 victory for St Helens at Swinton in 1953. However, even the most optimistic did not expect the record attendance of 42,793 set that day to be beaten. But both clubs were happy when a crowd of 26,074 poured into Central Park – 10,000 more than Wilderspool would have held.

The Lancashire Cup Final
Central Park, Wigan, 28 October
St Helens 26   Wigan 18

Traditionalists, irritated and ear-battered by the high-powered marching bands now used so often at important Rugby League matches, were pleased that the Pemberton Band, the genuine old-fashioned article, presented the pre-match entertainment.

The match began fiercely, and in the fifth minute Shaun Wane, the Wigan second rower, was penalized for a foul on the St Helens scrum-half, Neil Holding. Day's kick went wide. Three minutes later, Holding, switching play cleverly, swept a pass to Meninga – and it was a case of lighting the blue touch paper and retiring quickly.

Meninga, all sixteen stone of him, would not have been stopped by an elephant-gun as he crashed through mere flesh and bone in the corner. Day added a fine goal. In the tenth minute Wigan scored their first points, a penalty by Colin Whitfield after Peter Gorley had offended at a play-the-ball. Both Day and Whitfield each missed penalty kicks after, respectively, the Wigan captain, Graeme West, had made an improper tackle on Harry Pinner and several Saints defenders had been caught offside.

10   Sean Day, who started the season for St Helens as a trialist, settled in to become the league's leading goal-kicker in his first season. In the Lancashire Cup final against Wigan, Day struck five goals and made an important contribution to St Helens's victory.

There had already been hints that Saints were the stronger and more positive on attack, and it was just as well for Wigan in the seventeenth minute that their left wing, Henderson Gill, managed to slow down Paul Round after he had been put through a gap by Graham Liptrot's smart pass. Then Meninga hoisted a high kick and Vievers collected only to be held on the line. He took a knock, however, and two minutes later retired and was replaced by Roy Haggerty.

At last Wigan showed signs of threatening. Wane made a useful break and Wigan pressed keenly. Stephenson came away and passed to Cannon inside – should he have passed out to Ferguson on the wing? – who went close only to be penalized for a double movement as he tried desperately to touch down. Saints accepted this reprieve gratefully and immediately counter-attacked. Round seemed set to score when Ferguson, covering well, stopped him. But from the play-the-ball, Meninga raced in, drew the defence, and gave Haggerty the scoring pass.

Day's goal put St Helens ahead 12–2 after twenty-nine minutes. Pinner could even afford the luxury of an attempted drop goal; he missed, but it did not matter. In the thirty-fifth minute Meninga pushed off Jimmy Fairhurst, Ferguson and Stephenson before obligingly putting Day over in the corner. Day, equally obliging, added another excellent goal. A minute from half-time Meninga took a long pass, charged past the stand-off, Cannon, and left the full-back, Shaun Edwards, stranded, to score himself, with Day adding his fourth goal.

With a 24–2 lead Saints had little to worry about. Wigan, to their credit, made a contest of it through tries by Gill, West and Nicky Kiss – after Meninga had failed to hold a kick by Cannon, proving that he was human after all – and two goals by Whitfield. Day kicked a penalty for Saints to make the final score 26–18. Meninga strolled through the second half; he had done so much damage in the first half that it would have been cruelty if he had repeated the dose in the second. Even a Patagonian peasant would have picked him as man of the match.

St Helens: Vievers; Ledger, Allen, Meninga, Day; Arkwright, Holding; Burke, Liptrot, Gorley, Platt, Round, Pinner

Substitutes: Haggerty for Vievers after 22 minutes, John Smith not used

Scorers: tries – Meninga (2), Haggerty, Day; goals – Day (5)

The Burtonwood Brewery Lancashire Cup

Wigan: Edwards; Ferguson, Stephenson, Whitfield, Gill; Cannon, Fairhurst; Courtney, Kiss, Case, West, Wane, Potter

Substitutes: Pendlebury for Gill after 63 minutes, Scott not used

Scorers: tries – Gill, West, Kiss; goals – Whitfield (3)

Referee: R. Campbell (Widnes)

Attendance: 26,074

Jack McNamara

3

THE SILK CUT CHALLENGE CUP

The Challenge Cup competition, sponsored in 1985 for the first time by Silk Cut, had its most ragged start for years as the country was gripped by snow, sleet, frost and sub-zero temperatures from late January through to the middle of February.

The events of Sunday 27 January were a prelude and a warning that worse would follow. That was the day set aside for the preliminary round and, as so often happens, the draw had paired Leeds, one of the favourites, with Bridgend. At that time the luckless Welsh team had not won a game of any description. When their coach left Bridgend at 7.30 in the morning the players knew they were in for a rough time. It was already snowing heavily. They battled for eight hours through treacherous conditions to reach Headingley thirty minutes after the appointed kick-off time. After a warming cup of tea they ran out to a wonderful reception from 3,500 hardy spectators, a snowstorm, and a blizzard called Eric Grothe. The great Australian wing charged in for three tries as Leeds ran in thirteen touchdowns in a crushing 68–6 victory.

Bridgend deserved a bonus for completing the tie on a day when the only other fixture was in the second division at Southend. The weather relented to allow two other preliminary ties to be played two days later. Then Halifax, who had been one of the major importers of Australian talent, won at Barrow, while the second-division promotion challengers Salford beat the renowned cup fighters Featherstone Rovers.

When, on Sunday 3 February, Wakefield Trinity beat Doncaster in the other outstanding preliminary round tie, on a day when there was a full league programme, fears of more disruption by the weather seemed misplaced. It was an illusion. On the following weekend, the scheduled date of the first round, winter's fury brought chaos to the competition.

Leeds, with the benefit of their undersoil heating, were again able to play on the Saturday. But taking on the Challenge Cup holders, Widnes, in a televised tie was a very different proposition from thrashing Bridgend. A week earlier Leeds had won comfortably a league game at Naughton Park against a below-strength Widnes. There to see that victory was the Australian Malcolm Clift. He had arrived in England earlier that morning to take over as Leeds's coach from Maurice Bamford to enable Bamford to concentrate full-time on his Great Britain duties. The timing of the appointment was inappropriate to say the least. To change coaches and then take on the greatest cup team of the past decade is a recipe for disaster. Leeds looked as uncomfortable in the snow as Bridgend had done two weeks earlier. Their tactics indicated that they were playing neither to Bamford's plan nor Clift's and they lost their way in the snow.

Leeds could not handle the magnificent Widnes pack in which Kevin Tamati, back after a six-match ban, was outstanding. A winning margin of 14–4, with all the points coming in the first half, hardly reflected the control Widnes exerted.

The day after Widnes had made it clear that the trophy they had won so handsomely at Wembley the previous May would have to be prised from their grasp, just two more first-round ties took place. Halifax, having had to travel to one of the northern outposts at Barrow for a preliminary tie, now went on to one of the southern outposts, in arctic conditions, to win at Fulham.

The other tie to beat the weather was at Keighley, but the home club's efforts to make the pitch playable did not bring the anticipated reward for they were surprisingly beaten by Runcorn Highfield. The old Huyton club were delighted with their success and full-back Peter Wood deservedly claimed the glory, scoring all their points in a 12–5 victory.

Runcorn's ebullient coach, Geoff Fletcher, who had done more than anyone to keep the club alive over the years, rubbed his hands in anticipation at being in the second round, saying, 'I hope we are drawn at home to another second-division club which will give us a chance of making more progress.' However, his directors, mindful of the need for cash, had different ideas. They were hoping to be paired with one of their more affluent neighbours, Widnes or Warrington or St Helens, who had still to complete their games. Then Rugby League officials decided that, because so few first-round games had been completed, the second-round draw, scheduled for 12 February, would be postponed for a week.

The first round stumbled along with clubs arranging ties whenever their pitches became playable. Wigan borrowed Bolton Wanderers' football ground and hammered second-division Batley 46–8 on 17 February. Oldham also showed enterprise in making a similar deal with Oldham Athletic football club. The move misfired, however, for they lost 8–14 to Castleford.

When the second-round draw was made there were still seven first-round ties to be completed and there was the unusual situation of Wigan winning their way into the third round on 23 February with four first-round games still to be played.

Before then, second-division promotion rivals Salford and Swinton had shown it was not necessary to come from the upper reaches of the first division to produce exciting, entertaining rugby. Salford eventually won 31–6 but for almost sixty minutes supporters were treated to a nerve-tingling game as Salford clawed their way back from 0–6 down.

The same evening Rochdale beat second-division York 11–5 and then had to wait twenty-four hours to see if St Helens or Hull KR would be parading their skills at the Athletic ground. It was unfortunate that two of the game's outstanding clubs should be meeting in the first round. It was a tie many neutrals had hoped would be saved for a glorious sunny May day at Wembley.

There was a little touch of drama before the game. Rovers were delayed because of a mechanical fault with their coach and the kick-off was put back until 8 pm. However, it was well worth the wait, for the 10,000 crowd saw a magnificent old-fashioned cup-tie. In many ways it was a throw back to the game as it used to be played under the unlimited tackle rule. The tackling was fair but ferocious and it looked as though Saints might edge their way into the second round. With just nine minutes to go they were clinging to a 3–2 lead when the patient Rovers pounced. Swift passing out to the right gave the Great Britain winger, Garry Clark, just enough space to squeeze in at the corner and Fairbairn added a magnificent touchline goal.

Victory for Rovers finished Mal Meninga's dreams of playing in a Challenge Cup final at Wembley. The Australian centre had said that that was his ambition when he arrived in October and he had quickly repaid a huge piece of his signing-on-fee when Saints had won the Lancashire Cup.

Two days later two other Australians were keeping their dreams alive with performances of the highest quality. Wigan were determined to go back to Wembley to erase the bitter memories of their performance the previous May. Having destroyed Batley in the first round they faced opposition of a tougher kind at Wilderspool. Warrington were having an indifferent season in the league, having been hit by a series of serious injuries, particularly to their star three-quarter John Bevan and full-back Steve Hesford. They had, however, signed Widnes's Test scrum-half, Andy Gregory, only hours before the deadline, after he had looked certain to join his hometown club, Wigan.

The match provided all that is best in Rugby League – vigorous forward exchanges, sweeping attacks by speedy three-quarters and superb individual performances by Australians Brett Kenny and John Ferguson. We had first seen stand-off Kenny's skills in the autumn of 1982 when he toured Britain with the Australians. Then his sharp breaks and vivid acceleration were used as a finishing weapon. Now he was playing a more rounded game for Wigan.

The dazzling pace was still there, as was strength to take him through a tackle. But he was also a creator, varying his tactics superbly. Passes that went barely a yard were as effective as those sent several times that distance.

However, it was the wiry Australian on the right wing, John Ferguson, who was the hero of the chanting Wigan supporters. This was to be his final game before flying back to Sydney to take up his contract with Eastern Suburbs. Ferguson signed off in style with a glorious second-half solo try – his twenty-second touchdown in only twenty-four games – and was chaired from the field by his delighted colleagues after their 24–14 victory. But there was more to the Wigan display than a great Australian double act, for they had shown resilience and courage in fighting back from a 0–8 deficit half-way through the first half.

The game's most important cup competition would not be quite the same without the effervescent Alex Murphy. Murphy had been out of the game since the previous summer when he had been sacked by Wigan. On 22 February, two days before Leigh's five-times-postponed first-round tie with Huddersfield, he joined the Hilton Park club for the third time as team manager, John Woods keeping his place as player-coach. The appointment immediately raised speculation that Murphy, a four-times winner at Wembley, once with Leigh, could weave his magic again. Two days later Leigh duly disposed of second-division Huddersfield, but it was a victory without much merit.

That same afternoon Bradford Northern, Hunslet and Wakefield Trinity all beat the weather at last to fulfil first-round dates a fortnight late. Hunslet's 34–10 victory at Mansfield marked another milestone in the career of their plucky winger, Eric Fitzsimons. It was his first game for a year after breaking a leg. He hit five goals to top 1,000 career points.

Bradford, meanwhile, were crushing Southend Invicta 50–18 with the game's leading try scorer, Ellery Hanley, gathering another three touchdowns. But even Northern's half-century was not enough to make them the day's top scorers. Five second-round ties were completed, with Castleford thrashing first-division strugglers Workington Town 64–4. Hull, who ten days earlier had wiped out Carlisle 52–6 in the first round, gave a thoroughly professional display in winning 22–6 at Halifax. Here again another Australian, Test second-row forward John Muggleton, stamped his authority on the game, playing a prominent part in two tries and scoring the final touchdown.

Also cruising through to the third round that afternoon were Hull KR, Bramley, with a particularly fine win over Salford, and Widnes. Runcorn Highfield's directors had been granted their wish with a game against their neighbours Widnes. Unfortunately it was not at Runcorn's Canal Street ground but at Naughton Park. With half the Runcorn team coming from Widnes, coach Geoff Fletcher did not need to supply further motivation. Honest endeavour and 100 per cent effort, however, were never going to upset the Cup-holders, who won 36–11.

That left just two second-round ties to be completed during the following week, and both had provoked heated discussion. Great Britain were due to play France at Headingley on the Friday and there was a Colts international the following day. The result was that Bradford Northern had to tackle Wakefield Trinity on the Wednesday without Ellery Hanley and second-row Alan Rathbone, both of whom were in the British team.

Leigh, who played Hunslet on the Wednesday, were allowed to play Chris Johnson who had been named as sixteenth-man for Britain, but were told that Darren Beazant, Gary Hughes and John Westhead could not play against Hunslet because they were in the British Colts team on the Saturday. The position was clearly covered by Rugby League laws but Leigh were upset that Westhead could not play against Hunslet for he had been a regular first-team player.

Eight minutes after half-time it did not look as though it mattered. Leigh were on course for a third-round meeting with Hull Kingston Rovers. They led 22–4 and Hunslet were floundering. With sixteen minutes remaining Leigh were still in front 23–10 but suddenly the game started to run away from them. Inside five minutes Hunslet had smashed their way into a 28–23 lead as Leigh started to panic.

Hunslet's powerful Australian second-row forward, Mal Graham, scored the first try from a cheeky short kick to sow seeds of doubt in Leigh's mind. Two minutes later, when the ball bounced back from the crossbar from Graham's unsuccessful drop kick, Hunslet's substitute forward, Andrew Marson, scooped up the ball and plunged over. The surefooted Eric Fitzsimons added the goal to both tries and Leigh's advantage was now only a slender 23–22. Two minutes later it had disappeared as scrum-half Graham King raced forty yards to the posts. Again Fitzsimons added the goal and Hunslet were in front 28–23. There was still time for more drama for in the last minute the Leigh left wing, Phil Fox, raced in at the corner for his second touchdown. With John Woods out of touch with his kicking – he had landed a drop goal and a superb effort from near the touchline but missed others from much easier positions – the responsibility was passed to substitute Phil Johnson. He took his time placing the ball but although the direction was fine the ball dropped short of the posts. Hunslet ran off the pitch to celebrate a famous victory and a crowd-pulling home tie with Hull KR. Leigh trooped off dejectedly, shaking their heads and wondering how they had let a game, firmly in their grasp, be snatched from them.

Over at Odsal, Bradford Northern eased themselves through to a quarter-final match against Wigan with a 13–2 success over second-division Wakefield Trinity. Odsal Stadium, which had once housed more than 100,000 for the

Warrington–Halifax cup final replay in 1954, was undergoing a £1 million facelift. Accommodation and seating facilities were restricted and that prompted Wigan to suggest that the game be played at Central Park. Predictably, it was quickly rejected by Bradford's officials.

Odsal on 10 March presented an incredible spectacle. There was more than a passing resemblance to a building site. The stand on one side of the ground had long since been demolished. All that remained was a huge mound of earth dominated by a crane. Opposite there was a temporary stand with several rows of terracing in front. The scoreboard-end of the ground was in an advanced stage of development and was officially closed to the public. That left just one end of the ground to take the bulk of what turned out to be a 16,000 crowd, the best of the round.

They witnessed an enthralling and absorbing cup-tie in which luck favoured Wigan. Northern had their Australian prop forward, Bob Kellaway, limping after only eleven minutes, and nine minutes later their Great Britain hooker, Brian Noble, was also hobbling. A torrid quarter-final is no place for men struggling on one leg, and nine minutes before the interval Kellaway limped off to be replaced by veteran Charlie Stone. A minute later, as winger Steve Parrish was kicking Northern ahead with a forty-yard penalty, Noble also trudged from the pitch, to be replaced by centre Steve McGowan. These enforced positional switches certainly upset Northern for a time. McGowan went on to the right wing, Parrish switched to the second row of the pack, Dick Jasiewicz moved up to prop and Stone took on the hooking role.

By then the crowd was searching for more suitable vantage points. The steep soil banking behind the crane became dotted with scores of supporters while hundreds made their way to the scoreboard end of the ground. Several hundred took up positions on the speedway track while dozens more miraculously produced folding chairs and settled comfortably on the grass behind the goal. It was clear that the small number of police at the ground would have trouble removing them. A Northern official announced over the public address system that the referee, Kevin Allatt, would not restart the second half until the spectators had moved back behind the boundary wall.

They didn't budge, so Allatt took the only decision possible and got on with the game. Five minutes after the interval it did look as though the referee could have serious problems. Then Wigan surged ahead through the exciting Henderson Gill. Though many thought the ball was already out of play, and Gill himself perhaps offside, the Great Britain wing snatched up a Mike Ford cross-kick from under the nose of the Bradford full-back, Keith Mumby, and raced in for a touchdown.

Hundreds of delighted Wigan fans charged onto the pitch to congratulate Gill and to celebrate. That prompted another loudspeaker announcement telling the erring fans that Mr Allatt had threatened to abandon the game if there were any more pitch invasions. That, in my opinion, was the wrong tactic for it appeared to be an open invitation to spectators of the losing team to go onto the pitch. Then if Mr Allatt carried out his threat their team might have another chance to win.

Fortunately good sense prevailed. The fans, with some encouragement from a couple of mounted police, stayed off the pitch and Wigan got on with securing a place in the semi-finals. Ford increased Wigan's lead to 5–2 after fifty-three minutes when he thumped over a drop goal – with a touch of luck as the ball went in off an upright. Bradford teams are battlers if nothing else and two minutes later they were ahead. Ellery Hanley, the game's leading try scorer, produced a typically powerful run to create a try for McGowan. Parrish could not add the goal points and Northern's advantage was a tenuous one point.

Wigan's winning points sixteen minutes from the end again came from Gill, but this time from a thirty-five-yard penalty. Stephenson, a six-goal hero in the second round against Warrington, had missed with three shots and even though the club's leading goal-kicker, Colin Whitfield, was on the right wing, the ball was tossed to Gill. He had shown in a league victory over Hull KR a week before that kicking held no terrors, landing two wide-angled goals. This time it was a fairly straight shot and he sent the ball left-footed between the posts to back up his extrovert claim to be the best goal-kicker in the club.

The same afternoon those other first-division aristocrats, Hull Kingston Rovers, were cruising into the semi-finals with a 27–7 win over Hunslet. Just briefly, before and after the interval, Hunslet had looked capable of upsetting the Cup favourites. The veteran loose forward, John Wolford, prised open Rovers' defence eleven minutes before half-time and hooker Neil Gray combined to get the scrum-half King darting over near the posts. A drop goal from Gray three minutes after half-time cut Rovers' lead to 11–6. Unfortunately Wolford was not able to come out for the second half because of hamstring trouble and with his departure went Hunslet's hopes of victory. Rovers made their class and speed tell as they grabbed three second-half touchdowns from Clark, Robinson and Fairbairn.

Castleford left their indifferent and inconsistent league form behind as they swept through to their third semi-final in four seasons. It was a celebration day for the Beardmore twins, Bob and Kevin, as the second division's only survivors, Bramley, were crushed 58–18. Scrum-half Bob set up three tries in the first twenty-five minutes as Castleford took a grip they never relaxed. They went on to finish with eleven tries, three going to hooker Kevin, while Bob landed seven goals.

The other quarter-final between Hull and Widnes on the Saturday produced a hard, slogging battle which ended in a 6–6 draw, a war of words between club officials over the replay date and the inevitable club versus country dispute, because Great Britain were due to play France in Perpignan the following Sunday. Hull were handicapped by having to go into the match without their Kiwi three-quarter James Leuluai, who had broken a bone in the back of his hand ten days earlier, and Australian Test scrum-half Peter Sterling. Although Hull were able to bring in their former Great Britain international David Topliss at stand-off and switch Fred Ah Kuoi to scrum-half, the driving, organizing ability of Sterling was sadly missed.

Hull had most of the possession, exerted most of the pressure but could score only one try by Gary Divorty after fifty-nine minutes to which Crooks added the goal points. Widnes, with the exceptional pace of Lydon in the centre, counter-attacked inside four minutes with a marvellous long-range try. Deep inside his own half Lydon evaded the clutching hands of Steve Evans and raced almost fifty yards before serving his teenage wing partner Andy Currier. The Under-21 international could have taken the easy option and headed for the corner. Instead he turned inside, almost at right angles, completely wrong-footing the Hull cover, to put the ball down close enough to the posts to make Burke's goal-kick almost a formality.

That set up a replay and the squabble about the date and also left Hull with another injury problem for it was discovered that Ah Kuoi had a broken jaw and could not play for at least five weeks. Widnes wanted to stage the match on the Wednesday, Hull suggested Thursday, no doubt hoping the extra day would allow Sterling to recover. They also had the worry of international calls. After discussion with the League secretary, David Oxley, by telephone it was decided that the match would be played on the Wednesday. Having lost that battle Hull had another worry over which they had no control. Lee Crooks, Gary Divorty and Andy Dannatt were all in the Great Britain squad. The British coach, Maurice Bamford, was due to announce his team on the Tuesday and if any or all were in the team they could not be considered for the replay.

In the event Bamford selected Divorty as loose forward and Dannatt as travelling reserve. That meant that only Divorty was barred from the replay and prompted the Hull coach, Arthur Bunting, to say, 'I suppose it could have been worse, but nobody has done us any favours this season.'

The bad news was tempered by good news on the Wednesday, when Sterling declared himself fit. But it seemed of little consequence when Widnes went ahead within three minutes from a classic try. Hooker Kevin Tamati strode away from his own posts and galloped to within ten yards of half-way where fellow Kiwi Gary Kemble was waiting to tackle. Hull's fast wings, Dane O'Hara and the Welshman Kevin James, were also converging but Tamati timed his pass perfectly to the flying Joe Lydon. He revived memories of his two scorching tries at Wembley the previous May as he went on a diagonal run to the corner with James and O'Hara in vain pursuit.

Hull spent most of the first twenty minutes back-pedalling as accurate touch-kicks from John and Tony Myler drove Widnes forward. Gradually, however, Hull battled their way forward on the solid work of the front-row forwards, Skerrett and Crooks, fine work from the Australian second-row forward, John Muggleton and, inevitably, Sterling. Sterling's prodding and probing with a variety of kicks and passes emphasized how much he had been missed in the first game. Good combination by Muggleton, Leuluai and Schofield at last gave Hull a sound attacking position after thirty minutes and Sterling's perfect short pass allowed Evans to struggle over in a two-man tackle. Schofield's goal levelled the score.

Sterling, who had taken a knock earlier in the game, was again injured and disappeared to the touchline, returning sporting a bloodstained head-bandage and wearing a protective skull cap. Widnes again demonstrated those qualities which have made them the game's outstanding cup team to take a six-point lead just seconds from half-time. John Myler, who was a narrow winner of the man of the match award from Sterling, beat the onrushing Crooks fifteen yards from the line and made progress. Just when it looked as though the attack had faltered Myler slipped the ball to Keiron O'Loughlin who had to take no more than a couple of strides to score and the reliable Burke added the goal.

The first game at the Boulevard had been a slogging battle in which defences generally smothered attacks. Here, however, attackers had more room to display their skills. An unusual feature was the number of scrums, brought on by the use of accurate touch-kicking instead of high kicks to the full-backs which are invariably a waste of possession against such as Kemble and Burke.

With Shaun Patrick dominating the scrums Hull opened out play through the creative talents of Steve Norton and Sterling. Ten minutes after the interval Norton had a leading part in a four-man attack which squeezed O'Hara over in the left-hand corner to cut the margin to 10–12. The pressure mounted on Widnes for as they ran back to half-way to kick-off, Lydon limped out of the match with hamstring trouble. Widnes held out against a series of Hull attacks and it took a needless penalty to bring Hull level. The Widnes scrum-half David Hulme conceded the award at a play-the-ball and Schofield curled the ball between the uprights from thirty-five yards with just eleven minutes remaining.

Many thought that Hull had missed their victory chance in the first game. Now, however, they stayed the course better and Schofield was their match-winning hero. It was the Welsh right winger James, however, who caught the eye. Earlier in the season he had looked what he was, a tyro straight from Aberavon Rugby Union. Now his game showed remarkable improvement. He had scored excellent tries at Oldham in a championship game and in the second-

11   Hull's march to the final of the Silk Cut Challenge Cup at Wembley was prolonged by two important replays. In the quarter-finals, against Widnes, Hull won 19–12 after a 6–6 draw at the Boulevard; and in the semi-finals they beat Castleford 22–16 after a 10–10 draw at Headingley. Here, in the first quarter-final match against Widnes, Steve Evans tries to evade the tackles of Mick Burke (left) and Andy Currier

round victory at Halifax. Now it was as creator that he earned the adulation of his colleagues.

James was well positioned on the touchline when Burke drove the ball deep. Nevertheless, it still required a piece of high quality juggling before James could control the ball. He stepped inside the charge of John Basnett and went on a diagonal run towards the centre of the field. There, with his way blocked, he changed the direction of play with a turning pass which sent Schofield on a thirty-yard run to the right-hand corner.

Just to rub salt into the Widnes wounds the 19-year-old centre hammered a splendid touchline goal to stretch the margin to 18–12. And to make sure there was no way back for Widnes, Norton added a vital point from a drop goal with little more than a minute remaining.

Victory left all Humberside excited in anticipation of their two clubs meeting at Wembley; the draw, made two days before the replay, had paired Hull against Castleford and Rovers against Wigan.

The Challenge Cup Semi-final
Elland Road, Leeds, 23 March
Wigan 18   Hull Kingston Rovers 11

Colin Clarke, joint coach of Wigan, labelled this semi-final the punters' final. He was surely right, because all those thousands of uncommitted fans for whom a weekend in London in early May is an annual pilgrimage would have picked this pairing if they could have had a choice. The clubs had already played two splendid league games, with Wigan completing a fine double, but it was the second of these, at Wigan just three weeks earlier, that had everyone rubbing their hands in anticipation of a classic game at Elland Road. In that second game, Wigan, down 14–16 with only seconds to go, had won a thrilling match 20–16. That was a fine hors d'oeuvres, and although semi-finals have a reputation for being dour, sometimes downright dull, because the teams are too tense to play open football, no one expected Wigan or Rovers to make it a slogging forward battle down the middle.

The only problem for Clarke and his partner Alan McInnes concerned the right-wing position. Immediately after John Ferguson had flown back to Australia, Wigan had signed the Warrington international Phil Ford for £40,000 but he was cup-tied. They decided to recall the powerful Welsh international Brian Juliff for only his second senior game in five months. The regular goal-kicker, Colin Whitfield, was left on the bench and it was decided that David Stephenson and Henderson Gill would share the burden.

In a magnificent cup-tie full of high drama, Juliff repaid the faith of the Wigan coaches in the best possible way with the first try. Although Wigan dominated the opening twenty minutes they had nothing to show for all their effort until Juliff charged in for his touchdown after twenty-two minutes. He took his chance in style, hurtling in at the corner after a twenty-yard run and resisting a brave, crunching tackle from Fairbairn.

When Harkin dropped a goal for Hull KR five minutes later to leave the interval score only 4–1 in Wigan's favour it looked as if Wigan had missed their way, that they should have had more points for their first-half superiority. Hull KR's coach, Roger Millward, made inspired substitutions at half-time. He brought on the Kiwi scrum-half, Gordon Smith, for Harkin and the creative skills of forward David Hall for 'Zook' Ema. Millward won an instant dividend. Within two minutes of the restart Rovers were ahead. Hall created a half chance near the posts and Australian Gavin Miller's power and determination did the rest as he crashed over for a try. Fairbairn added the goal to leave Wigan trailing 4–7.

Four minutes later the margin had been clipped to a single point. Wigan were awarded a penalty on the left of the field, about thirty-five yards out. This time Stephenson successfully took the kick, following the planned policy of letting the right-footed centre have shots from the left of the field and those on the right being entrusted to the left-footed Gill.

In the following ten minutes the Wigan line took a pounding but, like Wigan in the opening twenty minutes of the game, Rovers had nothing to show for it. There are no prizes or points for near misses. As so often happens, it was a Hull KR near miss that was to provide the platform for Wigan to break out of defence and go ahead. Gordon Smith's short, diagonal kick over the Wigan try-line just rolled out of play with three attackers rushing in.

That gave Wigan the opportunity to restart with a tap on the '25' and there was no need to use their quota of six tackles to open the Rovers' defence. Graeme West charged through a big gap deep inside his own half. The tremendous stride of the tall Kiwi ate up the ground; he slipped by Fairbairn and turned the ball inside for Stephenson to cut in and score near the posts. Gill added the goal and Rovers, down 7–12, should have been deflated.

However, within six minutes the margin was back to a single point, but still in Wigan's favour, as a pulsating cup-tie had the 20,000 crowd hanging on every crunching tackle, every pass and kick. The skilful Hall created room on the right, handed on to Hogan, who sent a long, high pass out to the waiting Clark. Gill jumped to try to stop the ball but only succeeded in getting a minor deflection and Clark took the high ball at speed to hurtle over in the corner. Fairbairn failed with the wide-angled shot and that left Wigan clinging to a single point advantage.

With just twelve minutes to go, Wigan's Wembley dreams almost turned into a nightmare. Brett Kenny, who by his standards had no more than an average game, sent out a wayward pass on his own '25'. It went behind Stephenson and Gill and was scooped up by Garry Clark. He straightened up and had a clear twenty-yard path to the try-line. Wigan's substitute forward, Mick Scott, earned his winning bonus in that second. He took off in a flying dive to snatch the hem of Clark's shorts and it was enough to bring the winger to his knees.

Hull KR's last chance had gone and three minutes from time West confirmed his man of the match award when his high pass sent Gill over for the 100th try of his career and Stephenson added the goal points. Millward, talking about Scott's tackle, said, 'Just one inch stopped us going to Wembley. Wigan could not have come back if Clark had scored.'

Wigan's coach Colin Clarke agreed, 'It saved the day for us.' It left Wigan on course for the biggest-ever pay day at Wembley. Apart from their winning bonus their principal sponsor, former soccer star Dave Whelan, had guaranteed £1,000 a man for victory.

Wigan: Edwards; Juliff, Stephenson, Donlan, Gill; Kenny, Ford; Courtney, Kiss, Case, West, Wane, Potter

Substitutes: Scott for Wane after 43 minutes, Whitfield not used

Scorers: tries – Juliff, Stephenson, Gill; goals – Stephenson (2), Gill

Hull Kingston Rovers: Fairbairn; Clark, Robinson, Prohm, Lydiat; Mike Smith, Harkin; Broadhurst, Watkinson, Ema, Hogan, Kelly, Miller

Substitutes: Gordon Smith for Harkin and Hall for Ema at half-time

Scorers: tries – Miller, Clark; goal – Fairbairn; drop goal – Harkin

Referee: R. Campbell (Widnes)

Attendance: 19,275

The Challenge Cup Semi-final
Headingley, Leeds, 6 April
Castleford 10   Hull 10

A draw was the last result that either of these clubs wanted from a magnificent tie. It was no less than either club deserved but it added to the end-of-season fixture chaos, especially for Hull, and required an emergency meeting of League officials immediately after the game.

The replay date had been set for the following Wednesday at Headingley but Hull had fixtures scheduled for Monday (Barrow), Tuesday (Workington Town) and Thursday (Hull KR) while Castleford were due to play Halifax on the Monday and Oldham on the Friday. The League decided that the Monday fixtures must go ahead, gave Hull permission to postpone Tuesday's game and put back the Humberside derby until the Friday.

Both clubs were sharply critical of those decisions. The Hull vice-chairman, Peter Darley, said, 'We are not happy but have to accept it. I would have preferred Castleford and Hull being given a clear run to the semi-final replay and an extension to the season.' The Boulevard coach, Arthur Bunting, rapped, 'I am annoyed that a management committee can say you have got to play a league game before a semi-final of the greatest competition in the world.' Malcolm Reilly, the Castleford coach, said, 'I will be playing colts and 'A' teamers on Monday. It's a diabolical decision.'

Such acrimony could not devalue what had gone before. It had been a top-class cup-tie in which Castleford emphasized their right to be there. They started the game at breakneck pace and when the final whistle sounded, to the relief of thousands of Hull supporters, Castleford were camped on the Hull try-line. There were not too many flowing attacks but there were several fine individual performances which even the fierce tackling could not subdue. Hooker Kevin Beardmore set a wonderful example for Castleford. The creative skills which all had admired on the previous summer's Australasian tour were much in evidence but it was his domination of the scrums which had Hull back-pedalling for long spells.

Despite fine work by the half-backs, Orum and Joyner, Castleford's three-quarters never made the best use of all their extra possession. After repulsing the early storm it was Hull who took the lead after twenty-one minutes. Puckering, Sterling and Leuluai handled sweetly to give O'Hara a clear run to the line. Three minutes later the slick handling skills of Steve Norton and

65

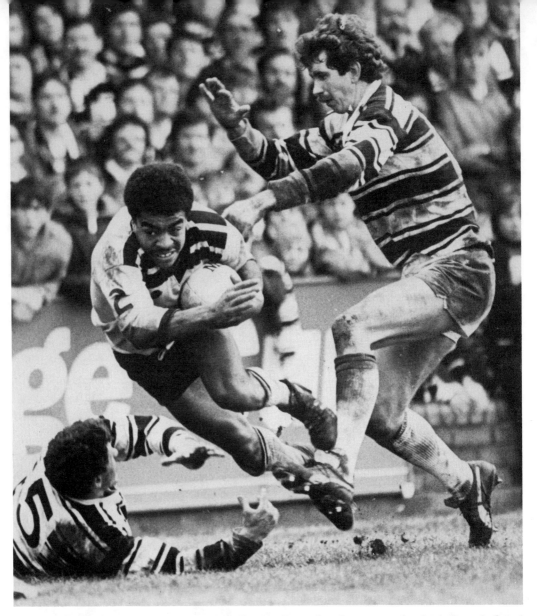

12 A draw, with a replay to follow, was the last result that Castleford and Hull wanted after a magnificent semi-final at Headingley in the Silk Cut Challenge Cup. Though fierce tackling by both sides put a stop to many flowing attacks, the game was played at breakneck pace. Here David Plange, the Castleford right wing, looks certain to be stopped by the Hull combination of O'Hara (left) and Evans.

Sterling opened up Castleford again and Crooks charged over at the posts. The referee, John McDonald, ruled out the touchdown for a forward pass, and after that escape Castleford showed that they too could handle with speed and skill.

Orum broke down the centre of the field and there was Joyner to take his pass and race thirty-five yards to the posts, holding off the challenge of O'Hara and Kemble. Hyde added the goal and eight minutes after the interval smart opportunism by Hyde brought a second touchdown. The Hull wing, Kevin James, was playing the ball a couple of yards from his own line with Schofield at acting half-back. Hyde, however, kicked the ball over the line and plunged in for the touchdown.

A 4–10 deficit was not going to be easy to overcome against a well-drilled Castleford defence and it took a typical piece of Sterling skill to find a way through after fifty-seven minutes. He hoisted a high kick, followed up to flick the ball to Muggleton, and when Muggleton's way was blocked five yards from the line he turned the ball back inside for Sterling to dive over. Scholfield, Hull's regular kicker, had failed with three shots so the captain, Crooks, took on the responsibility, and from a wide angle and in a difficult swirling wind curled the ball between the posts to level the scores.

Both teams had chances to win the tie in the later stages, Crooks with a penalty that went outside, and Castleford with a couple of try-scoring attempts which had Hull's hearts beating faster. It would have been rough justice if either team had been beaten, and while Sterling deserved his man of the match award for another non-stop display, Castleford had their heroes in Beardmore, Barry Johnson and Joyner.

Castleford: Roockley; Plange, Marchant, Hyde, Chapman; Joyner, Orum; Connell, Kevin Beardmore, Johnson, Nigel Wilson, Ward, England

Substitutes: Sigsworth for Orum after 45 minutes, Timson for Nigel Wilson after 48 minutes

Scorers: tries – Joyner, Hyde; goal – Hyde

Hull: Kemble; James, Schofield, Leuluai, O'Hara; Evans, Sterling; Skerrett, Patrick, Puckering, Muggleton, Crooks, Norton

Substitutes: Divorty for Puckering after 62 minutes, Topliss not used

Scorers: tries – O'Hara, Sterling; goal – Crooks

Referee: J. McDonald (Widnes)

Attendance: 21,013

The Challenge Cup Semi-final Replay
Headingley, Leeds, 10 April
Hull 22   Castleford 16

It was a mistake to blink in this dramatic replay, especially in the opening half. To do so was to miss a touch of skill, a defence-splitting pass, a try-saving tackle or, unfortunately, a vicious high tackle. The best memories are of six top-class tries, four to Hull and two to Castleford; the worst a series of high tackles, with both teams guilty, and an all-in brawl after the half-time hooter.

The tolerance of referee John McDonald stretched too far. A late, high tackle to the head by Ian Orum left the Hull full-back, Gary Kemble, prostrate after only ten minutes. He was helped from the field and took no further part in the game. Five minutes later, Hull's powerful Australian forward, John Muggleton, hit Gary Hyde with a tackle long after the ball had gone. Both offences brought penalties, but only mild rebukes, when, in my opinion, both offenders should have spent the rest of the match in the dressing-room.

Fortunately the bad and the ugly could not overshadow the good. There was another non-stop display from the world's best scrum-half, Peter Sterling, an outstanding game from James Leuluai and an inspirational lead from the Hull captain, Lee Crooks. There were passes of slide-rule precision from Steve Norton and the rich promise of the nineteen-year-old prop, Neil Puckering.

For Castleford, Kevin Beardmore emphasized that he is the best footballing hooker in the game, and the prop Barry Johnson, who had a hand in the build-up to both Castleford's first-half tries, again showed that he can handle the ball with the expertise of a top-class half-back.

It was Johnson and Beardmore, combining smartly after only two minutes, who sent Gary Hyde storming over the Hull line for the first try and the lanky centre added the goal to give his team a dream start. That score and the loss of Kemble stung Hull into retaliation and they equalized after eighteen minutes with a glorious try. Divorty, Leuluai – now at full-back – Sterling, Puckering and Crooks handled in a sweeping fifty-yard attack for O'Hara to race in at the corner.

Crooks calmly added the goal from the touchline to equalize, and three minutes later Hull were ahead. Sterling, with a typical Australian 'bomb', had Castleford's defence in a tangle and there was the great Kangaroo star to gather the ball and plunge over for Crooks to kick the goal which pushed his team into a 12–6 lead.

The frantic pace never slackened, but it was Castleford who now revealed the

13   The slick handling skills of Steve Norton and Peter Sterling were thorns in Castleford's side during the first Challenge Cup semi-final at Headingley. Here Steve Norton gets a pass away to Kemble, the Hull full-back.

ability to attack from long range. Johnson and Beardmore combined in a forty-yard break down the middle. Hull halted the attack close to the posts, but before their defence could regroup Roockley linked up from full-back to take Hyde's pass and plunge over. With Hyde again landing the goal to level the score there had been 24 points in as many minutes.

In the ten minutes before the interval Hull snatched two more tries to build a convincing 22–12 interval lead. Topliss, Crooks and Muggleton combined to send the right wing, Kevin James, racing over the line and the Welshman cut in sharply to present Crooks with an easier target. Surprisingly, Crooks failed with the kick but he more than made amends two minutes from the interval. Then, playing the best football of his career, Crooks timed his short pass perfectly to send Leuluai speeding through from forty yards. He rounded Roockley, and three despairing defenders could not stop a score which was conceived and executed perfectly. Crooks's third goal left Hull sitting comfortably on a 10-points lead, an ideal cushion for the second half.

69

It was too much to expect the second half to continue at the same blistering pace. Tired limbs and bruised bodies lost their sharp cutting edge. Hull tightened their defence and Castleford could not produce the skill or pace to create one clear-cut chance until the last minute. Then Chris Chapman put the finishing touch to fine work by Plange and Marchant, but Hull's army of support was already in full voice with their victory anthem heralding another trip to Wembley, their fourth in six seasons.

Hull: Kemble; James, Schofield, Leuluai, O'Hara; Evans, Sterling; Crooks, Patrick, Puckering, Muggleton, Norton, Divorty

Substitutes: Topliss for Kemble after 10 minutes, Edmonds for Puckering after 71 minutes

Scorers: tries – O'Hara, Leuluai, James, Sterling; goals – Crooks (3)

Castleford: Roockley; Plange, Marchant, Hyde, Chapman; Joyner, Orum; Ward, Kevin Beardmore, Johnson, Nigel Wilson, Timson, England

Substitutes: Reilly for Nigel Wilson after 39 minutes, Sigsworth for Orum after 47 minutes

Scorers: tries – Hyde, Roockley, Chapman; goals – Hyde (2)

Referee: J. McDonald (Widnes)

Attendance: 21,017

The Challenge Cup Final
Wembley Stadium, May 4
Wigan 28   Hull 24

Five days after one of sport's greatest occasions, the final of the Challenge Cup at Wembley, referee Ronnie Campbell received an award as 'referee of the year'. Campbell was asked what it was like to be involved in a match of such magnificence, played before a record crowd. He is not normally stuck for words to describe any situation, but all Ron could say was, 'It was magic.'

14 One of the outstanding players of the 1984–85 season was John Ferguson, who not only made a huge contribution to Wigan's successful season in the league but scored two magnificent tries in their Challenge Cup final win. Here Ferguson scores what proved to be the winning try, thrusting past Lee Crooks's tackle.

It may not have been magic but it was the closest Rugby League will get to it. Fortunately, the quality of the rugby is on record for future generations on BBC Grandstand film. In years to come it will be necessary to prove that descriptions of it in fading newspaper cuttings and in dog-eared books are not fantasy. It was my twenty-ninth Rugby League final at Wembley and it surpassed anything I had seen in the other twenty-eight. There were several superlative individual performances which were still part of outstanding team displays.

Inevitably the Australians Brett Kenny and John Ferguson of Wigan and Peter Sterling of Hull demanded and commanded the centre stage. When Kenny stood around with his hands thrust into his track-suit pockets at the pre-match formalities I thought we would either see a display which would reach for the stars or go to the other extreme and be a flop.

Kenny looked unconcerned, indifferent, and maybe even a little bored with the ceremony. For fifteen minutes little was seen of him as Hull bombarded the Wigan line and took a 2–0 lead with a Lee Crooks penalty in the first minute which was extended to 6–0 with a well-conceived and executed try by Kevin James after ten minutes.

Then we had seen Kenny's Parramatta club-mate and half-back partner Sterling reveal his strength. Sterling shrugged off an attempted tackle by Donlan, slipped the ball to his brother-in-law, John Muggleton, and Gary Kemble linked up from full-back in magnificent style. Kemble dragged three Wigan defenders out to the touchline before switching the ball inside to James who had a clear path to the line.

Hull should have had more than one try to show for all their early pressure. Crooks's failure to add the goal to James's try did not look important at the time. At the final reckoning the Hull captain's three failures from five shots and substitute Garry Schofield's two off-target attempts were to prove vital.

Gradually Wigan battled their way out of a deep defensive position, and sharp attacks on either wing provided a warning to Hull of how and where Wigan intended to strike. Ferguson was given half a chance on the right and Kemble did well to halt the flying wing ten yards from the corner flag after fifteen minutes.

Within seconds the point of attack had been switched to the left and again Kemble's faultless tackle stopped left-winger Henderson Gill with a textbook defence. When Wigan switched the focus of attack again we saw the skill of Kenny for the first time. He made a diagonal run to the right and although held in a two-man tackle he got the ball away to Ian Potter. Potter emphasized how much his game had improved. Mainly noted for his defence, the rangy loose forward threw a perfect long pass to the waiting Ferguson. Ferguson was like a tightly coiled spring waiting to be released. He shaped to come inside Dane O'Hara but then in half-a-dozen strides had swept round the outside for a top-class try to which Gill added an equally fine goal to level the scores.

Ferguson, along with his wife Sheryl, had arrived in Britain from Sydney only five days before but that one try made their air fares a bargain. That score was the start of one of the finest attacking spells I have seen in any level of rugby. It brought back memories of the great Australian touring team of 1982 and it was no coincidence that Kenny and Sterling, key members of that team, now on opposite sides, again had the key roles.

Wigan surged to a 28–12 lead ten minutes after half-time. In those thirty-four minutes 34 points were scored, all 28 of Wigan's and just another 6 to Hull. Leading Wigan's charge to what appeared an invincible lead was Kenny. After twenty-five minutes he scored a dazzling solo try following a curving forty-five-yard run. His nineteen-year-old partner, Mike Ford, provided the chance with a long pass of exquisite timing. Kenny's vivid acceleration did the rest and I do not remember anyone going around Kemble on the outside the way the Australian did. Following their policy of switching kickers according to which

15 Henderson Gill, Wigan's left wing, scored a magnificent try, hurtling over the line after a sixty-yard dash, in the Challenge Cup final at Wembley and was a constant source of danger to Hull. Here he is tackled by Sterling (left) and Kevin James before he can inflict further damage.

side of the posts the tries were scored, Stephenson added the goal from the left to nudge Wigan ahead 12–6.

Seven minutes later Crooks landed his second goal from a close-in penalty award to clip the margin to four points. But with less than two minutes to the interval Wigan again revealed that they are at their most dangerous when attacking from long range. Deep inside their own '25' they launched an attack which brought one of the season's outstanding tries. As the move developed the noise from Wigan's red and white army of 40,000 supporters built to a crescendo. Ford, Kenny, with another perfectly weighted and timed pass, and Stephenson set Gill free on the left.

The chunky Gill set his sights on the try-line sixty yards away and took a perfectly straight course as the despairing Kemble tried to cut him off. The Kiwi got close and in fact managed to get his hands to Gill's ankles, but nothing was going to stop him hurtling over the line and producing a mile-wide grin.

With a 16–8 interval lead Wigan were in command and Sterling said after the game, 'Everything starts with defence and we did not get that right. We had dug ourselves a hole at half-time and we could not get out.' Three minutes after the break Hull were in more trouble. A quick heel from a scrum on Hull's '25' gave Kenny another chance to stamp his authority on the game. He took Ford's pass, shaped to go outside, changed direction, stepped out of Sterling's tackle and up came another of Wigan's talented teenagers, the full-back Shaun Edwards, to take the pass and race in at the posts.

Another Gill goal and Wigan had stretched their advantage to 22–8. Now it looked as if they would romp to one of Wembley's biggest-ever victories. Within three minutes, however, Sterling had gained some revenge. He wrong-footed half-a-dozen Wigan players, including Kenny, on a scything, diagonal run to the right. He again revealed his strength, for as Edwards made the tackle a couple of yards from the line Sterling flipped the ball inside for Steve Evans to touch down.

Crooks again failed with the goal-kick and Wigan's 10-point lead stretched to 16 five minutes later. The unlucky O'Hara, the one wing not to get a clear running chance, was unmarked on the left but dazed after stopping Stephenson with a crunching tackle. Sterling's long pass had O'Hara in trouble. He fumbled the ball, slipped and there was Ferguson swooping to pick up the ball and race unopposed forty yards to the line, curving in to make Gill's goal-kick that much easier.

That really should have been the end of Hull. Wigan took off the limping Brian Case and replaced him with Danny Campbell, and Hull substituted one teenage forward, Neil Puckering, with another, Gary Divorty, and brought on their leading goal-kicker, Garry Schofield, in place of O'Hara whose vision had been affected by slight concussion.

Hull, however, refused to lie down. Sterling was where the action was hottest. Their loose forward, Steve Norton, again emphasized that his handling skills are equal to anything Australia can produce. Lee Crooks set an inspiring lead and it is hard to believe that he is still only twenty-one.

After sixty-four minutes Shaun Patrick, Norton and Rose handled to give Leuluai a simple touchdown. Again Crooks failed with the goal attempt but Hull regained the attacking rhythm which had all but disappeared after the opening fifteen minutes. Little had been seen of Leuluai but he created space for Schofield to bring the best out of Edwards's defence. With just seven minutes to go Hull's flickering hopes burst into life as Sterling's sharp pass sent Divorty diving over. This time Schofield curled the ball the wrong side of the upright.

Now the difference was just eight points and with five minutes to go Wigan's defence was ripped apart by Leuluai. He took Fred Ah Kuoi's pass forty-five

16 The two outstanding players in the enthralling Challenge Cup final at Wembley were the Australians Brett Kenny (Wigan) and Peter Sterling (Hull), both members of the Parramatta club in Sydney. Though Kenny deservedly won the Lance Todd Trophy as the outstanding player on the field, Sterling gave a virtuoso performance which would have won him the award in any other year.

yards out and at speed. Leuluai changed direction without breaking his stride and once past Edwards a try was the only possible outcome. Again Schofield missed the goal-kick but the margin was now only four points; Wigan were wilting and Hull were eager to get on with the game.

But Wigan survived. Kenny won the Lance Todd Trophy by a landslide margin, the first Australian to claim the honour, and told me later, 'Those final minutes were the longest of my life.' Kenny, Ferguson and Gill grabbed the limelight for Wigan. Ford revealed outstanding potential at scrum-half, and

Edwards again showed the vision which will make him a permanent fixture in international teams for the next decade. The attacking opportunities for the thoroughbreds were all made possible by the honest craftsmen in the pack – Graeme West, who set a fine example, Ian Potter and the solid Neil Courtney.

It was impossible not to feel sorry for Hull. They had scored five tries, the same number as Wigan, and had made a massive contribution to the most enthralling, exciting final I have seen. Sterling gave a virtuoso performance which would have won him the Lance Todd Trophy in any other year. Norton, Crooks and Muggleton formed a sound base on which to build a victory. Sadly a victory which had looked theirs for the taking disappeared because they could not control Kenny nor stop Wigan setting free their outstanding wings.

Hull's coach, Arthur Bunting, said, 'It is no consolation to be told that we have taken part in a great, maybe the greatest final. I would have preferred to have played badly and won.' One can understand his feelings, especially as this was Hull's fourth visit to Wembley in six seasons with not one victory.

Jubilant Wigan left the stadium almost three hours after the final whistle. Their heads were held high. They smiled and waved to their supporters. The memory of their dreadful performance the previous May had been erased. Graeme West said, 'We wanted to come to Wembley, play well and win well and repay our magnificent supporters.' That they did in a style I shall never forget.

Wigan: Edwards; Ferguson, Stephenson, Donlan, Gill; Kenny, Ford; Courtney, Kiss, Case, West, Dunn, Potter

Substitutes: Campbell for Case after 56 minutes, Du Toit not used

Scorers: tries – Ferguson (2), Kenny, Gill, Edwards; goals – Gill (3), Stephenson

Hull: Kemble; James, Evans, Leuluai, O'Hara; Ah Kuoi, Sterling; Crooks, Patrick, Puckering, Muggleton, Rose, Norton

Substitutes: Schofield for O'Hara and Divorty for Puckering after 58 minutes

Scorers: tries – Leuluai (2), James, Evans, Divorty; goals – Crooks (2)

Referee: R. Campbell (Widnes)

Attendance: 99,801

Alan Thomas

4

THE SLALOM LAGER CHAMPIONSHIP AND PREMIERSHIP TROPHY

THE SLALOM LAGER CHAMPIONSHIP

Hull Kingston Rovers held firm when it mattered most to win the Slalom Lager Championship for the second successive season. It was an outstanding triumph and a tribute to the depth of talent in the Rovers squad. They put together lengthy winning runs to launch and then sustain their challenge and survived the demanding end-of-season rush, when a glut of fixtures tested stamina to the full. Their success meant that the title has remained on Humberside for the last three years. Rovers became the third team to win the title in successive seasons, following Swinton in 1963–64 and Bradford Northern in 1980–81, and the first to win it three times.

The cut and thrust of a league campaign has probably never been better illustrated than it was in 1984–85. The leadership changed hands continuously. At the turn of the year St Helens, Hull Kingston Rovers, Wigan, Oldham, Leeds and Widnes were separated by only two points. In mid-February Rovers came from behind, thanks to two remarkable tries by winger John Lydiat, to snatch a crucial win at Leeds and move four points clear. But their lead was always threatened for they were still involved in the Challenge Cup, and the see-saw nature of their challenge was emphasized when, a month later, Rovers were five points adrift of Leeds but had six matches in hand.

In the end Hull KR might well have felt that they had won the league title in a match they had lost against Wigan, at Elland Road, Leeds, in the semi-final of the Challenge Cup. They were beaten in a thrilling encounter and hopes of a

77

league and cup 'double' were dashed, leaving that possibility still open to Wigan. But Wigan, facing that awkward run-up to Wembley, encountered a savage programme of matches. Injuries took their toll and inevitably the thoughts of some players centred on the Cup final and individual performances faltered. Moreover, the modern game, with the handover of possession after six tackles, brings fewer scrums and makes it increasingly difficult for teams to play two or three matches a week.

After their semi-final success Wigan promptly faced three matches in five days, at home to Oldham and away matches against Hull and Leeds. It was soon obvious that the championship was not to be theirs and they were beaten in the away games to emphasize the fact. Rovers, meanwhile, adjusted rapidly to league demands after the cup setback, helped by a quick return to Elland Road four days later to meet relegation-haunted Hunslet. A crushing 42–14 victory, with Gary Prohm scoring four tries, was the ideal tonic and after another four days a second 40-point win, at home to Barrow, confirmed their recovery.

After those healthy wins, Hull KR could now take a cool look at the task facing them. With Wigan out of the running, the opposition was going to come from St Helens, Leeds and Oldham but all three had already played many more matches. Thus Rovers' destiny was in their own hands. They did not need teams above them to drop points for they had sufficient games in hand to overtake all three. Only visits to Hull and St Helens stood out like jagged teeth to cause possible snags. Here again fate took a hand. The game against Hull, due to be played on Good Friday, was called off because Hull had to play a Challenge Cup semi-final the following day.

When Hull and Castleford drew their semi-final and had to replay the following Wednesday, Hull were set to face Rovers on the Friday, having played two ferocious cup-ties less than a week earlier, with a near-reserve team sent to Barrow in between. The game was very much a low-key affair. Hull suffered a flood of injuries, played the entire second half with twelve men and even Craven Park fans were muted in their celebrations. They prefer derby fixtures to be keen affairs on Humberside.

Two days later, Rovers were at St Helens but played a much-weakened side and Mal Meninga scored a second-half hat-trick of tries as Saints won comfortably 30–14. Rovers, however, had judged the situation perfectly. They knew they could afford the defeat at St Helens as long as they made certain of their other matches. Three days later they romped to a 53–8 win at Halifax, then beat Bradford Northern at home and clinched the title with a 30–14 success at Barrow with a match to spare. They had won seven out of eight games in eighteen days. Later, they were to be joined in the struggle for the Premiership Trophy by St Helens, Wigan, Leeds, Oldham – all of whom had contested the lead at the beginning of the year – and Hull, Widnes and Bradford Northern.

Hull Kingston Rovers' triumph was all the more satisfying because they shook off the loss of second-row forward Chris Burton, who broke his ankle at Wigan in early March. Burton's strong play had been an important part of the pack. He is the sort of player who keeps opponents on edge and had returned from the Lions' summer tour to Australia a much-respected figure. His loss was a real blow and certainly affected their cup hopes but in the league players such as Phil Hogan, Roy Holdstock and John Millington stepped up to maintain momentum.

Prop Mark Broadhurst was again the rock on which the pack was built. 'Zook' Ema learned much from Broadhurst during the season and David Watkinson revelled in his new role of captain. Rovers also discovered another of those unknown Australians who, from time to time, emerge to make a massive impact in Britain: this time it was Gavin Miller, who proved a tremendous acquisition. Fiercely competitive, he also showed many subtle touches and was a much better handler than many supporters realized. He slotted perfectly into the pack when he was tried at loose forward.

An early-season injury to Gordon Smith gave Paul Harkin another chance at scrum-half which he duly accepted, doing well enough to force his way into the Great Britain squad. Rovers have long been admired for the quality of their approach work and the finishing touches were often clinically applied by centre Gary Prohm. Prohm always seemed to be in the right place at the right time and only Ellery Hanley's remarkable efforts at Bradford Northern prevented Prohm gaining much greater recognition for a record-breaking season at Craven Park.

The runners-up, St Helens, were left pondering some odd away performances, such as a thrashing at Castleford and a draw at Halifax. They had lost two matches, one at Hull Kingston Rovers, when Meninga arrived. The big Australian centre proved the massive draw the club had hoped for when they signed him. Moreover, he brought with him a very capable player in Phil Vievers and Knowsley Road began to buzz again. But it was by no means an exclusively Australian success. Loose forward Harry Pinner played some superb rugby, showing immaculate timing in his passes, and scrum-half Neil Holding was frequently eager and elusive.

There was a period around November–December when St Helens positively dazzled in the league and their 48–16 victory over a Leeds side, who were playing well themselves, contained high-speed rugby of rare quality. Barry Ledger continued to be a dangerous winger with good pace, and on the other flank Saints discovered a highly efficient goal-kicker in Sean Day, who started as a trialist and settled in to become the league's leading kicker in his first season. Day played his part as St Helens amassed a new first-division points record of 920, an astonishing total in these days when extra concentration on defence is supposed to restrict scoring potential.

There was also notable effort at Knowsley Road from the often underrated Roy Haggerty, the sort of utility player all teams should possess, and the young forwards Andy Platt and Paul Forber continued their development. Prop Tony Burke was an ideal front-row forward, giving sturdy support when the occasion demanded in a thoroughly consistent year.

As with Saints, it was good to see the crowds returning to Wigan's Central Park. A healthy 20,012 saw the Good Friday game against St Helens and throughout the season the fans were rarely disappointed. Wigan also moved shrewdly into the Australian market and returned with stand-off Brett Kenny, a wonderfully accomplished player, who played a major part in knitting the side together. Kenny had a natural eye for an opening and proved an ideal link between backs and forwards. Like Meninga, he produced tremendous response from the players around him.

Wigan also brought over an Australian winger, John Ferguson, who was relatively unknown in Britain. He provided the excitement that Central Park supporters expect from their wingers and had scored twenty-two tries when he returned home in February to meet contractual obligations with his club, Eastern Suburbs. When Ferguson left, Wigan bought the exciting Phil Ford from Warrington, to prove that they were willing to provide the spectacle that supporters at the club had come to regard as a right.

Ferguson's fellow winger, Henderson Gill, reacted favourably to the challenge of having such an exciting player on the other flank and he too found a high level of consistency to score more than thirty tries in the season with some devastating running. Gill was full of self-confidence and also gave some substance to his claims to be the best goal-kicker at the club when Colin Whitfield lost the job.

Wigan's pack was solid and effective, well led by Graeme West, with Shaun Wane developing rapidly, while at scrum-half Mick Ford proved an exciting prospect under Kenny's influence.

Leeds caused a good deal of astonishment and attracted criticism by recruiting no less than ten overseas players, nine Australians and the New Zealander Trevor Clark. Unfortunately they arrived at different times over a period of three months and this inevitably meant constant team changes. But with injuries affecting so many of their home players, Leeds would have been hard pressed even to survive in the first division without their overseas players, let alone finish fourth.

Injury during the previous summer's tour of Australia meant that the Great Britain prop, Keith Rayne, made only two substitute appearances all season, and his twin Kevin played just six full games after breaking his arm early in the season. Further injuries to Roy Dickinson, Ian Wilkinson, Kevin Squire, John Holmes, Gary Moorby, David Ward and the Australian Rickie Lulham, who were all out for long spells, meant there was little competition for places and the confrontation between British and Australian players at the club which many cynics forecast did not materialize. This was partly because of the commonsense approach of coach Maurice Bamford. But not long after the beginning of the season Bamford was claimed by Great Britain and the club felt obliged to ease his workload and appointed the Australian coach Malcolm Clift in February.

Leeds's outstanding Australian was Eric Grothe, considered by many to be the best winger in the world, but not always appreciated, apparently, by the other Leeds players. Grothe did not make his debut until 1 January, when he scored a hat-trick of tries. But generally the service he received was utterly inadequate and too often fans were left feeling frustrated at the waste of such talent.

There was a wholehearted stint from prop-forward Trevor Paterson, who was voted player of the year by the supporters. The Australian Test second-row, Fullerton-Smith, took time to settle as he tried to adjust to a more free-running role than he had been accustomed to at home. Gavin Jones was an exciting player but suffered more than his share of injuries. The real surprise was the centre, Tony Currie, another Australian hitherto unknown in Britain, who proved a player of high quality and was good enough to persuade the club to invite him back for another season.

One amazing fact came out of the season at Headingley. Even with the arrival of Grothe, no fewer than fourteen players turned out on the wing, a statistic difficult to accept for supporters who had grown accustomed to the old firm of Alan Smith and John Atkinson.

Oldham's season, not for the first time, promised much but never quite developed, despite their respectable fifth position. They had enormous pack potential in Andy Goodway, Mick Worrall, Terry Flanagan, Mick Morgan and Alan McCurrie and were strengthened by the Australian Chris Phelan in the forwards and by Paul Taylor in the backs. The backs never really carried the fire power that is expected from a leading side and their overall points total was well short of those in the top four. Goodway missed a number of matches through injury and illness and was subsequently transfer-listed at £100,000 after another Great Britain tourist, David Hobbs, had been signed from Featherstone. There was a further unhappy period when scrum-half Ray Ashton and loose forward Flanagan asked for transfers, the former making strong public criticism of Oldham's style of play.

Hull's season in the league never got off the ground as match after match had

81

to be postponed because of various cup commitments and international calls. They had made a moderate start, losing four of their first six matches. When they went down at home to Leeds on 5 December, making five defeats in nine games, their title hopes were virtually extinguished. A team with title ambitions cannot carry more than six defeats and Hull already realized that their fixture pile-up would put them out of the running.

With a strict deadline imposed on clubs because of the demands of the Premiership Trophy, matters came to a head in late season, when Hull quite seriously pondered the idea of playing two games in a day. This was frowned on by the League and they eventually settled for three games in three days.

Peter Sterling's return to the club was greeted with justifiable enthusiasm and he fulfilled all hopes with some magnificent performances, often producing his best in big matches. He proved a great ambassador around the schools, an asset some clubs were slow to take advantage of so far as their Australians were concerned.

Arriving with Sterling from Australia was the second-row forward John Muggleton, whose ability to appear in the right place at the right time brought him a number of tries. Garry Schofield and Fred Ah Kuoi had their seasons affected by injury, and prop Trever Skerrett struggled manfully to find his old rugged form after a much-delayed return from a bad knee injury. Lee Crooks thrived after being appointed captain, despite his youth. It did not escape notice that some of his most constructive displays came at open-side prop, a position many feel may yet prove to be his best. Hull achieved a shrewd signing in Welsh winger Kevin James, who showed a speed and alertness that quickly endeared him to the supporters and soon put him among the tries.

There is still a strength in depth at the Boulevard that few clubs can equal. This was underlined late in the season when, because of fixture congestion, Hull had to field some apparently hopelessly weakened teams and still achieved remarkable results. They, like their neighbours Hull Kingston Rovers, look set for a long run among the elite.

After eleven seasons of outstanding success, Widnes had to settle for a period of adjustment. They were also forced to operate for a considerable time without stand-off Tony Myler, still suffering from the knee trouble that dogged him on the previous summer's tour to Australia. Joe Lydon, of whom much was expected after his dazzling Wembley success the previous season, also had one of those seasons when injury took a toll. Widnes's problems were further heightened by the dispute which kept Andy Gregory away from the club for several months before his transfer to Warrington in a part-exchange deal, which brought forward John Fieldhouse to Naughton Park. Further forward strengthening came with the signing of the New Zealand Test player Kurt Sorensen; with fellow New Zealander, Kevin Tamati, in lively form, the forwards carried a distinct threat.

However, the absence of so many class backs had a detrimental effect, although a bright wing prospect was discovered in Andy Currier, who scored some spectacular and important tries. There was good effort at times from David Hulme at scrum-half and John Myler was a reliable player in a variety of positions. Veteran hooker Keith Elwell was released on loan to Barrow for a time but at the end of the season was still as sprightly as many players in the first division.

The fact that Bradford Northern finished in the top eight with a limited squad, and were much respected in the knock-out competitions, speaks volumes for the spirit at Odsal. Naturally Ellery Hanley provided the highlight of the season, with his fifty-five tries. It was sad, though, that he had to operate so often at a stadium that resembled a building site as that huge bowl at Odsal underwent an extensive facelift. Centre Steve McGowan had a splendid first half of the season and there was typical effort from Jeff Grayshon, who failed again to get to Wembley, and Dick Jasiewicz. Loose forward Alan Rathbone was an impressive figure in a number of matches and gained an international place. But once again he began to stay away from the club and was badly missed later in the season.

Northern sprang a major shock in the week prior to the first round of the Challenge Cup by announcing that coach Peter Fox would not be retained when his contract expired at the end of the season. The timing of the announcement was staggering. It created unrest among the players and sparked a petition among the supporters but the directors held firm. They owed much to Fox over the years for his ability to make the best of severely limited resources and in general his record with the club had been exceptional. The decision to appoint Barry Seabourne as his successor was reward for his tireless efforts with the Odsal Colts team, but he faced a demanding task.

There was further consternation among the Odsal supporters when hooker Brian Noble was allowed to leave early for his stint in Australian club rugby. This may have been a fine gesture to Noble, but with his stand-in, Chris Preece, injured, the side were left to struggle in the closing weeks of the season without a recognized hooker.

Featherstone Rovers just missed the Premiership play-offs and for a team with so little in reserve this was a very creditable effort. Again, they played virtually the whole season without the desperately unlucky loose forward Peter Smith, who made a brief comeback in March.

A fire which destroyed most of the main stand at Post Office Road added to the club's already serious financial problems and they launched an appeal for funds. A gift of £50,000 from West Yorkshire county council eased some of their problems and Test forward David Hobbs was sold to Oldham near the end of the season for £40,000, thus providing another windfall.

Scrum-half Deryck Fox was the outstanding Rovers player. He had an excellent season and followed a distinguished line of scrum-halves at the club by gaining full Great Britain honours. Stand-off Andy Mackintosh, on loan from Leeds, gradually regained the form which had made him such an exciting prospect two years earlier and the signing of such promising local players as Neil Woolford and Brian Waites was a pointer to the future. So, too, was the form of the young loose forward, Paul Lyman, who had a good season in difficult circumstances.

Halifax followed, and finally overtook, Leeds in the signing of Australian players. President David Brook made no bones about the fact that he felt this was the only way to ensure first-division survival. He said that outstanding British players were simply not available for the money he had paid for the Australians. Nor did he believe that their commitment and dedication equalled that of the Australians he had bought. No fewer than ten Australians played in the team in some matches and when they met Leeds there were more Australians on duty than British players.

Not everyone was happy with this situation and the sacking of coach Colin Dixon, a popular character at Thrum Hall, and the appointment of Chris Anderson, another Australian, as player-coach, created an awkward situation. Some British players openly expressed their dissatisfaction, and one outcome was the transfer of John Carroll to Batley for £10,000. However, Halifax's final run to the John Player semi-finals, and a great effort against Hull KR, soothed many feelings.

Another previously unheard of Australian, scrum-half Michael Hagan, a player of good build, pace and strength, made an enormous impact at Halifax and returned with a high reputation. The young loose forward, Paul Langmack, also enjoyed a marvellous season and there was sterling work from Keith Neller and big Martin Bella.

Unfortunately off-the-field problems continued and the players were rebuked by Mr Brook at one stage. But his point was made when Halifax stayed in the first division. Also satisfying was the fact that attendances, which started at 1,800, settled around the 4,000 mark. The difficulty for Halifax now is to consolidate that success and the Australian market must continue to look tempting.

The positions of Warrington and Castleford, two much-respected teams, just above the relegation zone reflected their disappointing league seasons. Both could be fiercely competitive and Castleford came within an ace of reaching Wembley, but generally both were far too brittle when the occasions demanded a totally committed approach.

Warrington emerged with little credit when they signed Steve Diamond,

Hussein M'Barki and David Allen, after Fulham's players had been declared free agents by the courts. A signing which was much better received and created great excitement at Wilderspool was that of scrum-half Andy Gregory, from Widnes. He is a controversial player but has skill and is capable of lifting a team. He arrived perhaps too late to influence matters fully but did enough to whet the appetite. The subsequent search for forwards of real stature underlined the fact that the club were well aware that Gregory needs cover and support.

A disappointment to many fans was the transfer of the mercurial Phil Ford to Wigan. He and fellow winger Brian Carbert, a promising youngster, gave genuine pace and flair to the three-quarters. The absence of Great Britain centre Ronnie Duane for most of the season was a heavy blow. His strength and pace in the middle were badly missed. And another severe handicap was the prolonged absence of Steve Hesford. Warrington were happy to see their versatile Australian back, Paul Younane, give good service in various positions, but overall it was a low-key year for them.

It was typical of Castleford that while they were entertaining great hopes of Wembley, they had equally strong fears of relegation. On their good days they owed much to hooker Kevin Beardmore, and the fact that he was leading try-scorer with fifteen tells its own story. The injury to Beardmore's twin, Bob, at a vital stage left a huge gap that was never filled.

John Joyner showed some clever touches but no one could decide whether his best position was loose forward or stand-off and numerous switches did not help the team's rhythm. Castleford recruited Australians in utility back Ron Sigsworth and second-row forward Nigel Wilson. They gave useful service without becoming the commanding figures the side needed.

When a reserve team was called upon to play a senior fixture against Halifax a few days before Castleford's Challenge Cup semi-final against Hull, it was interesting to see two sons of famous Castleford fathers on the field. Ian Hardisty played at stand-off, with his father Alan the opposing physio, and Ian Hartley, son of prop Dennis, made an appearance as substitute.

The only surprise among the four teams relegated was Leigh, who after holding their own for some time, were sunk by a dreadful mid-season spell of eleven successive defeats. The long absence of Test winger Des Drummond, and injury to player-coach John Woods, meant a drastic reduction in the club's points-scoring abilities. By the time an old Hilton Park favourite, Alex Murphy, took over as coach from Woods, relegation was virtually assured. Murphy was quick to realize that the forwards had little to offer, and he may well need the breathing space of a full season in the second division to put Leigh back on the map. Full-back Chris Johnson did well enough in a lost cause to catch the eye of the Great Britain coach Maurice Bamford. There are other capable young players in John Westhead, Gary Hughes and Darren Beazant, but a good forward leader is essential for them.

Barrow had rampaged through the second division the previous year but found life entirely different in the top bracket. The retirement of Ian Ball, and injuries which wrecked Andy Whittle's career and ended Steve Tickle's season early added considerably to their problems. In mid-season their coach, Tommy Dawes, expressed the club's frustration at being unable to attract quality players to the area. Centre Dave Heselwood and prop Andy Sykes were bought from Leeds but it was not enough. Despite a sad lack of cover, scrum-half David Cairns was rarely overshadowed and deserved a better fate than relegation.

Hunslet were aware of their problems from the outset as their defence collapsed in alarming fashion. They had a tendency to fade late in a game and a 40–41 home defeat by Barrow after leading 40–29 in the closing minutes was typical. Recruiting attempts met with only limited success and Barry Banks, leased from Hull, broke his leg after barely three months at the club.

The old master craftsman, John Wolford, was persuaded to play one more season for Hunslet and duly obliged. Even at his deceptively-casual pace his handling skills were still good enough to confuse many defences, but he needed aggressive support and his season ended early with injury. Hunslet's talented scrum-half, Graham King, was not overawed in top company and collected fifteen tries, showing rare pace. Hunslet were another club to turn to Australia for extra strength and had prop Gerry Byron, second-row forward Mal Graham and centre David Murray in their ranks.

Graham proved to be one of the finds of the season. He showed all the qualities expected of an Australian back-row forward and, apart from some solid tackling, provided a bonus by becoming the club's top try-scorer with seventeen. Hunslet were naturally keen for him to return, but having paraded his skills at top level he was reluctant to return to second-division rugby and had already attracted the attention of leading clubs. Hunslet blooded some capable young forwards in Andy Bateman, Mark Wood, Kelvin Skerrett and Chris Bowden, while hooker Neil Gray tried hard. But, handicapped by injury, Hunslet had to play as many as five loan players in some of their important late-season matches. Ironically, with their cause lost, Hunslet went to Wigan and won. Then they came down to earth, losing their last two games at St Helens and against a weakened Hull side, conceding 126 points in the process.

Workington also found that life at the bottom of the first division was much tougher than life at the top of the second. Their season was a disaster. They conceded 40 points or more in five of their first seven league matches and this set the pattern as they gained only two wins and a draw in thirty matches. The side was humiliated when losing 4–64 in the second round of the Challenge Cup at Castleford and conceded 60 points in league games at St Helens and at home to a scratch Hull team. Clearly the days when Cumbria was an area where visitors feared to tread are long gone and all four of the county's clubs settled in the second division with the failure of Carlisle and Whitehaven to win promotion.

Centre John Jones brightened some of the Workington games with his spirited running, and stand-off David Smith and prop Gary Nixon had their moments, but the club was hopelessly ill-equipped to cope with a return to the first division. The so-called attraction of first-division rugby also proved a myth as supporters refused to watch a losing team. Derwent Park did not draw a crowd of more than 1,500 all season, a desperate state of affairs for a club seeking to survive let alone thrive.

The second division was a hotch-potch. The admittance of Mansfield Marksman and Sheffield Eagles brought an unwieldy number of twenty clubs and meant an imbalance of fixtures. Various solutions were suggested and finally a divisional system was agreed giving a total of twenty-eight league matches.

Fortunately Dewsbury did not win the title, otherwise there might well have been demands from across the Pennines for a top-four play-off to settle officially the destination of the second-division championship and the Slalom Lager prize of £9,000. The honour and the cash went to Swinton. They had shown towards the end of the previous season that they were ready to make a strong challenge and this soon proved to be the case.

Swinton were a well-balanced team with a number of good young players. They were also fit, a tribute to the dedication of the coach, Jim Crellin, and this fitness proved an important asset in several matches when they came from behind to win. The club was sensibly managed too. Aware of the dangers of a fixture pile-up, they were ready to play a 'home' fixture against Sheffield Eagles at the Bolton Wanderers' football ground in mid-January when the weather was especially bad, and were rewarded with a crowd of nearly 1,500.

Scrum-half Martin Lee had an outstanding season. He and the fast wingers, Derek Bate and Ken Jones, all reached the twenty-try mark and there were sound contributions from Jeff Brown, Les Holliday and Steve Snape. The second-division title was all the more gratifying for Danny Wilson, still a much-respected player, after an injury-troubled first half of the season had prevented him from playing as often as most supporters would have liked.

York never seemed to claim much attention but, after losing four of their first nine matches, they moved steadily up the table and two lengthy winning runs eventually brought them promotion. They relied heavily on the all-round talents of stand-off Graham Steadman, who beat York's twenty-seven-year-old record for the number of points in a season when he registered 318 from twenty tries, 116 goals, and six drop goals. He also beat his own record for the highest number of points in a match when he scored 26 in the 54–4 home win over Batley. Salford achieved one slightly surprising distinction by becoming the only one of the four teams relegated the previous season to bounce straight back to the first division. Ged Byrne underlined the team's pace with some fine finishing to follow up his encouraging season in the first division a year earlier. Darren Bloor had some excellent games at scrum-half and the club found a fast winger in Ian Marsh, who scored a hat-trick of tries on his debut.

Marsh helped to fill the gap created when the Australian winger Steve Stacey suddenly flew home after a mixed stay. He scored six tries, earned a three-match ban and was fined £100 by the team manager, Kevin Ashcroft, on one occasion for missing the team coach. Salford paid a record £16,000 for the Wigan loose forward, John Pendlebury, and Clive Griffiths, signed on loan from St Helens, also proved a shrewd acquisition, scoring tries and landing vital goals. The side's potential was shown when they gave Wigan a fright before going down in the Lancashire Cup semi-final and they played particularly well to beat Featherstone in the Challenge Cup, going on to thrash Swinton before losing at Bramley.

Dewsbury were a surprise packet, having finished fifth from bottom the previous season. Their coach, Jack Addy, had done his groundwork well during the summer to bolster a developing young side. The experienced forward Dave Busfield was leased from Hull and was joined by the New Zealand centre, Chris Mita, and the Australian Tony Murphy. All three were to play important roles in the surge for promotion at the end of the season.

Mita was a tremendous find. Very strong on attack, he brought the best out of the other backs, notably his fellow centre, Paul Jennings. The New Zealander was also sound in defence and Crown Flatt followers learned with relief that Dewsbury had snapped him up for a further two seasons. Murphy started at stand-off in the second team but his tackling quickly attracted attention and he was moved to the pack, taking over at number 10. Dubbed the 'tackling machine', his tackle count was more than fifty in several games.

The two new clubs, Sheffield Eagles and Mansfield Marksman, began with the usual burst of optimism and encouraging attendances only to see interest fade, the bad-weather break not helping. Sheffield relied mainly on a mixture of seasoned professionals. Their old hands included player-manager Gary Hetherington, props Billy Harris and Vince Farrar, and loose forward Paul McDermott, on loan from York. But they also signed some promising teenagers from amateur clubs. The New Zealanders looked useful but had to leave early for home, and although Sheffield created interest with the signing of Steve Redfearn, attendances dipped as results were disappointing. They also had to cope with the collapse of their main financial backers, Telvista Television.

Mansfield had the advantage of starting on a good pitch at Mansfield Town's soccer ground, Field Mill, and player-coach Mick Blacker built his squad on hardened Rugby League experience. Derek Finnigan and Mike Kelly, from Warrington, half-back Terry Langton, centre Steve Nicholson and hooker Carl Sanderson were important acquisitions and prop Dave Chisnall was also signed for a three-month spell.

Mansfield made an encouraging start, winning nine of their first ten league matches, and attendances held up well for the first half of the season. Indeed, they led the table for a time and even looked a good promotion bet. However, when they lost form and started to slide down the table, attendances fell too and Mansfield and Sheffield joined the worrying number of second-division clubs where attendances are too often around the 500 or 600 mark.

There was considerable concern regarding Fulham, Southend Invicta (formerly Kent Invicta) and Bridgend (formerly Cardiff), all of whom had to move grounds. Fulham, taken over by the enthusiastic Roy Close, transferred to the Crystal Palace recreation centre, but were savagely hit when a number of players declared that the change of ownership made them free agents and won backing from the courts. In the circumstances Fulham did remarkably well to make any sort of progress. They were bolstered by the now customary influx of Australians, of whom Mike Davis, especially, enjoyed a good season at half-back and Don Duffy showed courage and dedication in defence. Steve Mills collected his share of tries and Fulham could reflect on a season in which they had at least held their own, when a less determined club might have surrendered. It was soon apparent that the vast national recreation centre was altogether unsuitable for Rugby League. Attendances of 700 to 1,000 were lost in the great bowl and spectators were much too far away from the playing area. Late in the season some matches were played at the Wealdstone football club ground to suggest that another move might be on the cards. Eventually, during the summer, it was announced that the Central London Polytechnic ground at Chiswick would be Fulham's home during the 1985–86 season.

Bridgend and Southend had nightmare seasons. The Welsh club resumed without such well-known names as Steve Fenwick, Tommy David, Paul Ringer and Brynmor Williams, and played on the Bridgend Town football ground. Although centre Mike Davies gained Welsh international honours against England at Ebbw Vale and looked a useful player, the side was woefully weak even for the second division. In the last two months the situation became farcical when Bridgend turned up at Dewsbury twenty minutes late for an 8 pm start with no less than thirteen trialists among the fifteen on the team sheet. The list included their new owner Eugene Caparros, who went on as substitute to make his Rugby League debut at the age of thirty-nine, a commendable effort but not to be recommended. Notice to quit the Coychurch Road ground added to Bridgend's desperate situation. If Rugby League is ever to gain a hold in Wales it must be of a high standard and this was not the case in 1984–85.

Southend Invicta's venture at the local football ground was a disaster. The move had alienated those who had developed a feeling for the code when the club had been based at Maidstone. Locals showed only passing interest and four wins all season did not help. In the last weeks of the campaign the only interest in Southend's fortunes was in seeing how low the attendance could drop and the last fixture's 'crowd' of around 100 for the home game with Huddersfield was truly appalling.

Huyton's switch to the Runcorn football ground under their new name of Runcorn Highfield brought increased attendances and better results, and more than a touch of respectability to the club. Peter Wood's feat in playing and scoring in every match was a magnificent effort and Ian Smith and Brian Garritty led the way in try-scoring. The season ended on a sad note when that great optimist and enthusiast, Geoff Fletcher, ended his remarkable playing career.

Doncaster, so often Runcorn's companions in distress, appointed another new coach in John Sheridan from Castleford and he used his contacts to strengthen the team. Injuries at times left the squad threadbare, but though there were alarming results there were also signs of encouragement. Not least was the appointment of nineteen-year-old full-back Kevin Harcombe as captain. Harcombe gained Great Britain Colts honours and showed great maturity in his play. Matters were clearly improving at Tatters Field, though sadly this was not reflected in attendances, and after two wins and an away draw – amazingly at York – the club faced another financial crisis in having to pay out so much winning money.

Wakefield Trinity and Whitehaven experienced low-key seasons after relegation. Trinity began with Geoff Wraith as coach, changed to David Lamming, and ended with the former Great Britain captain, Len Casey, in charge. Casey had no time to make much of an impact but will certainly demand more dedication. There are some capable young players such as Nigel Bell, Ian Hopkinson and Gary Spencer but many of the others were not good enough. However, the bright spot at Belle Vue was the success of Trinity's Colts team, all of whom have now signed as professionals.

Ten wins out of their first eleven matches suggested that Whitehaven might stroll back to the first division, and an international cap for Vince Gribbin gave the club great satisfaction. But there was a bad mid-season spell and the Cumbrians quickly lost their promotion hopes.

Carlisle shook off the memories of two years of struggle with a spirited season which took them close to promotion. Gary Peacham equalled the club's try-scoring record of twenty-five, Kevin Robinson and Kevin Pape were also among the tries and Dean Carroll, signed on loan from Bradford Northern, solved their goal-kicking problem. Initiative was shown in the signing of Milton Huddart, from Whitehaven, for a five-figure fee, and of the impressively quick John Stockley from Blackpool. The club also showed enterprise in forming a second team, playing at Penrith, and their disappointment in relatively modest attendances was understandable. They deserved better as promotion hopes died only in the last fortnight.

Batley changed coach in mid-season, with George Pieniacek taking over to launch a charge of fourteen wins from their last seventeen league matches. Centre Carl Gibson equalled his own post-war club record of twenty-six tries and gained Great Britain honours, suggesting that Batley might well be challenging for honours in 1985–86.

Blackpool Borough had their moments, not least a Lancashire Cup win at Oldham and an England cap for their prop Hugh Waddell. Sadly, his season ended soon after with a broken leg. Andy Bailey impressed at full-back, Norman Turley landed his usual tally of drop goals, and their new signing, Tommy Frodsham, equalled the club record of four tries in a game in the win over Bridgend. But Blackpool's inconsistency did not satisfy the demands of their coach Tommy Dickens.

Rochdale Hornets, Huddersfield and Bramley all changed coaches, with Charlie Birdsall, Chris Forster and Ken Loxton respectively taking charge. All three will be hoping for better luck than their predecessors. Keighley, too, had a season with little to cheer. All in all the second division continues to give cause for concern, with an unwieldy structure, indifferent playing standards, and mostly poor attendances.

THE PREMIERSHIP TROPHY

St Helens's great victory in the Slalom Lager Premiership final robbed Hull Kingston Rovers of a hat-trick of trophies and spread the honours more evenly after Humberside had threatened to scoop the pool. St Helens were rewarded for inspired approach work and lethal finishing and were able to raise their game when the pressure was on.

However much this competition is criticized because of the demands that a fixture deadline imposes on clubs, it invariably produces some of the season's most entertaining rugby. As often happens, the first round was relatively low-key. Wigan's match against Hull at Central Park only a week before their Wembley meeting had the edge removed when Hull opted for caution and played only three of their eventual Cup final team. Wigan, however, were in no mood for complacency and crushed Hull 46–12. Phil Ford again showed what a lively replacement he will be for the Australian John Ferguson, with four tries. There were two for Gill as well.

St Helens started slowly against Widnes at Knowsley Road and might well have been caught out had early breaks by Tony Myler and Hulme found the right support. Widnes generally looked ponderous and once Pinner's pass enabled Platt to break the deadlock there was only one winner. Pinner sent Holding in for a second try and at 12–0 at the interval Saints were through. Their second-half task was made easier by the dismissal after forty-nine minutes of Tamati for using his elbow, and a 26–2 scoreline was fair reflection of their superiority.

The Leeds v. Oldham game promised to be close and swung on the dismissal of Oldham hooker McCurrie for kicking. At that stage Leeds held an uncertain 8–0 lead and were only 8–2 at the interval. But they settled things quickly in the second half. Paterson earned the man of the match award before going off with a rib injury which cost him a semi-final place, while Hunt underlined his quality as a full-back and Currie looked very sharp at centre. The 36–18 score stemmed from a late frolic on Oldham's part.

The champions, Hull Kingston Rovers, were always in control against Bradford Northern at Craven Park. Of particular interest were Prohm's two tries which enabled him to equal the record for the number of tries for a centre set by Tommy Gleeson of Huddersfield in 1914, while Northern's Hanley took his season's tally to fifty-five. Prohm also figured in tries by wingers Clark and Laws before Rovers killed off a brief Northern rally, second-row forward Kelly scoring three tries in the last fifteen minutes.

**The Premiership Trophy Semi-final
Craven Park, Hull, 1 May
Hull KR 15   Leeds 14**

Drop goals are a relative rarity from Rovers' full-back Fairbairn but he landed three that proved crucial. Leeds scored three tries to two but Creasser missed with three shots at goal. It was ironic that in the last seconds Dick took over the kicking and landed a touchline goal.

Rovers had more of the play but their early confident handling faltered against the determined tackling of Bleakley and Webb and mistakes mounted in the strong wind. They had to settle for two Fairbairn drop goals and trailed 2–4 at the interval. Grothe, who doesn't need a following wind to be dangerous, had ignored Clark's attempted tackle to score at the corner and make it clear that Rovers had a fight on their hands. Fairbairn's third drop goal narrowed the gap but Leeds went 8–3 ahead when Dick and Holmes paved the way for a picture try by Currie.

A significant first-half change for Rovers had been the introduction of Harkin at scrum-half for the injured Gordon Smith and he used the wind to drive Leeds back with a series of well-judged kicks. Rovers still needed a big effort and a scrum heel gave Mike Smith the chance to create a good attacking position. A move appeared to have broken down on the last tackle but the ball was re-gathered and a lobbed pass sent Laws over near the posts.

Leeds lost the dangerous Currie through injury and Rovers pressed strongly. Reward came when substitute Lydiat dodged three defenders, Fairbairn provided the link and Mike Smith dived over. Fairbairn's goal gave Rovers the cushion of a 15–8 lead. It was needed. Leeds launched a last-ditch attack through the talented Medley, and Creasser forced his way over. Dick's towering goal set Rovers' nerves jangling but the hooter brought instant relief.

Rovers were in their second successive final and Leeds were left pondering three semi-final defeats during the season, on all three Humberside grounds at the Boulevard, Boothferry Park and Craven Park.

Hull Kingston Rovers: Fairbairn; Clark, Robinson, Prohm, Laws; Mike Smith, Gordon Smith; Broadhurst, Watkinson, Ema, Kelly, Hogan, Hall

Substitutes: Harkin for Gordon Smith after 32 minutes, Lydiat for Clark at half-time

Scorers: tries – Laws, M. Smith; goals – Fairbairn (2); drop goals – Fairbairn (3)

Leeds: Hunt; Hague, Creasser, Currie, Grothe; Holmes, Dick; Dickinson, Maskill, Jones, Webb, Heron, Bleakley

Substitutes: Hill for Dickinson after 23 minutes, Dickinson for Hill at half-time, Medley for Currie after 63 minutes

Scorers: tries – Grothe, Currie, Creasser; goal – Dick

Referee: M. R. Whitfield (Widnes)

Attendance: 7,137

The Premiership Trophy Semi-final
Knowsley Road, St Helens, 8 May
St Helens 37   Wigan 14

The epic Wembley final three days earlier and its aftermath took its toll on Wigan. St Helens showed superior teamwork and, not surprisingly, appeared the more hungry for success. Pinner orchestrated matters and the unsung Ainsworth and the promising Platt responded with great zest, while Meninga made his awesome presence felt. However, Wigan made them battle, despite the fact that their mainspring, Kenny, was almost anonymous. Mike Ford, Kiss and the irrepressible Gill always had the Saints on edge.

Meninga set things moving after eighteen minutes when his perfectly-delayed pass enabled Peters to send Arkwright over, Meninga adding the goal. Wigan levelled when Kenny was seriously involved for the only time in the game. He served Dunn and Stephenson dummied his way over. Gill's goal was followed by a Stephenson penalty and Wigan were ahead. Meninga, who often seems to be only in second gear, suddenly became super-charged. Ledger caught Wigan flat-footed when he took Phil Ford's kick deep in his own territory and made good ground. Meninga supported and showed surprising pace for a big man in holding off Phil Ford and Juliff and thundering fifty yards to the line. A Pinner drop goal sent Saints in 11–8 at the break and their supporters began to sense a St Helens win.

Pinner struck again when he took Arkwright's pass and galloped thirty-five yards to the line and Ledger's goal seemed to make Saints safe. Gill clearly thought otherwise. His weaving run sparked an intricate move in which he and Campbell figured twice before Phil Ford raced over. Stephenson added the goal and gave Wigan hope at 14–17 with only fifteen minutes left.

94

17 Harry Pinner, the St Helens loose forward and captain, was the deserved winner of the Harry Sunderland Trophy as the outstanding
player in the final of the Premiership Trophy at Elland Road, Leeds. His
swift breaks and clever passing were major factors in St Helens's 36–16
victory over Hull KR.

However, hope faded to a glimmer as Ledger eased Saints with a penalty goal and they finished with a flourish. The energetic Ainsworth finally broke Wigan with a well-earned try and further tries scored by Allen and Holding finished them off. The scene was set for another spectacular final.

St Helens: Vievers; Meadows, Peters, Meninga, Ledger; Arkwright, Holding; Burke, Ainsworth, Gorley, Platt, Haggerty, Pinner

Substitues: Forber for Burke after 10 minutes, Allen for Peters after 38 minutes

Scorers: tries – Arkwright, Meninga, Allen, Pinner, Ainsworth, Holding; goals – Ledger (5), Meninga; drop goal – Pinner

Wigan: Phil Ford; Juliff, Stephenson, Donlan, Gill; Kenny, Mike Ford; Courtney, Kiss, Campbell, Dunn, West, Potter

Substitutes: Du Toit for West after 48 minutes, Whitfield not used

Scorers: tries – Stephenson, Phil Ford; goals – Stephenson (2), Gill

Referee: F. Lindop (Wakefield)

Attendance: 18,500

The Premiership Trophy Final
Elland Road, Leeds, 11 May
St Helens 36   Hull KR 16

Beware the sleeping giant for when he stirs there is danger. The part played by St Helens's great centre, Mal Meninga, in the final may not have been as consistent as that of the man of the match Harry Pinner, but it was dramatic and swung the issue.

Meninga scored two tries, each an interception from the luckless Hall. His first was a mere canter over forty yards to take Saints 22–10 ahead after thirty minutes, his second settled the match. Rovers had fought back to be only 16–22 down after sixty-three minutes and were giving St Helens a tough time, when

18   The Australian full-back Phil Vievers, who joined St Helens with Mal Meninga, was another comparatively unknown Australian to make his mark during the 1984–85 season. Here he scores one of St Helens's first-half tries in the final of the Premiership Trophy.

Meninga loomed up to take Hall's pass in his own '25'. He looked like a run-away bus but, as in the semi-final, again showed exceptional pace to hold off Fairbairn and the speedy Clark for his try. From that point Saints were safe and pressed home an advantage they had always seemed to hold over a highly-suspect Rovers defence and registered the highest score in a Premiership final.

Hull KR had done well to shrug off injuries to Burton and Miller in the late title run and reach the final but their absence was keenly felt at Elland Road. Saints gave early notice they could create openings and Haggerty made at least four breaks without reply from Rovers. Pinner's clever passes helped to set up tries for Ainsworth and Vievers, with fine supporting play from colleagues.

Rovers might well have had an argument regarding forward passes. But they had left ominous gaps in their defence and had no answer to a superb piece of rugby by Ledger which brought the third St Helens try. Though not at their best Rovers were still in the hunt. Fairbairn dodged over from a scrum to cancel out Ainsworth's score and Hogan collected Watkinson's kick for Prohm to send Laws over before Meninga struck for the first time. A lovely dummy by Broadhurst, head and shoulders the best Rovers player, enabled Robinson to score and at 14–22 at the interval Rovers were by no means dead.

The tackling on both sides tightened in the second half and it took a Fairbairn penalty goal to give Rovers a much-needed score. They brought on Harkin for Gordon Smith but this time he was unable to work a miracle and, like his colleagues, could only watch Meninga's broad back disappearing when the centre intercepted for the second time.

Pinner swerved in for the sixth Saints try, just in time to influence voting for the Harry Sunderland Trophy as the game's outstanding player. More classic play, featuring Holding and Allen, enabled Ledger to race in for the final score. Wembley was a hard act to follow but Saints came close to achieving it.

St Helens: Vievers; Ledger, Peters, Meninga, Day; Arkwright, Holding; Burke, Ainsworth, Gorley, Platt, Haggerty, Pinner

Substitutes: Forber for Burke at half-time, Allen for Meninga after 77 minutes

Scorers: tries – Meninga (2), Ledger (2), Ainsworth, Vievers, Pinner; goals – Day (4)

Hull Kingston Rovers: Fairbairn; Clark, Robinson, Prohm, Laws; Mike Smith, Gordon Smith; Broadhurst, Watkinson, Ema, Kelly, Hogan, Hall

Substitutes: Lydiat for Ema after 48 minutes, Harkin for Gordon Smith after 61 minutes

Scorers: tries – Fairbairn, Laws, Robinson; goals – Fairbairn (2)

Referee: S. Wall (Leigh)

Attendance: 15,518

Trevor Watson

5

FIVE PLAYERS OF THE SEASON

Selecting five 'Players of the Season' is an onerous task, like tipping the first five in the Grand National. What follows is purely a personal choice and, pondering the list, it would probably have been easier to pick just one player or to widen the choice to ten in order to include some deserving cases, who have just missed out.

The decision of British clubs to import so many top-class Australians and New Zealanders inevitably meant that they dominated the season and would figure prominently in any list of five best players. But there were certainly candidates from the less publicized second division. It was, for example, very difficult to omit Runcorn's Peter Wood. His club record of 240 points (4 tries, 98 goals and 28 drop goals) and his achievement in playing and scoring in every match during the season deserves mention on its own for his club won nothing. York's Graham Steadman, another to have created a club record, was also a candidate but at least he has the chance to show his talents in the first division next season. Sadly, and it is a special regret, I have to omit Gary Prohm, who in any other season during the past twenty years would have stolen the scoring limelight.

I hope my final choice will meet with some agreement. At least it should stimulate discussion in a sport that during 1984–85 showed why many regard it as the greatest game in the world.

Trevor Watson

Ellery Hanley (Bradford Northern)

Ellery Hanley made himself an automatic choice during a phenomenal season which brought him no less than fifty-five tries. He was an outstanding member of Great Britain's touring party to Australia and New Zealand the previous summer, and returned from it a stronger and more confident player. When he reached the half-century of tries to become the first man to achieve the feat since Billy Boston in 1962, there was relief as well as delight, for it was felt in many quarters that the days of such individual feats were over. Hanley's tally included seven matches in which he scored three tries and two others in which he collected four. For good measure he also landed thirty-six goals.

19   In a phenomenal season Bradford Northern's Ellery Hanley scored an astonishing fifty-five tries, breaking the record held since 1962 by Billy Boston. A beautifully balanced player, with strength and lightning acceleration, Hanley scored a hat-trick of tries in no less than seven matches, four tries in two other games, and for good measure kicked thirty-six goals.

So often players start well on firm grounds but fade when the heavier conditions arrive. Hanley began in a blaze of tries and maintained momentum, despite the fact that Northern were not the strongest of teams. Two of his hat-tricks came in matches when his side were beaten. A beautifully balanced player, many of his tries stemmed from lightning acceleration and strength in breaking the tackle, others from intelligent support of breaks by such forwards as Jeff Grayshon and Dick Jasiewicz. He also created tries for others.

Hanley was a throwback to the days when people went to matches to watch particular players. It was a measure of his appeal that more than Bradford Northern supporters were roused when he was in possession. As the big Australian clubs gathered for his signature to a contract Hanley showed good judgement in deciding to have a summer's rest.

Peter Sterling (Hull)

Peter Sterling's success was one of the season's lesser surprises. He had shown his outstanding ability during Australia's 1982 tour of this country and added to his reputation during an all-too brief period at Hull during 1983–84. There was astonishment in Britain when he failed to gain a Test place against the 1984 RL Lions in his own country. When he arrived at the Boulevard again he promptly dispelled fears that this was due to any loss of form: it had clearly been a case of Australian misjudgement.

The complete craftsman, Sterling invariably reserved his best displays (there were no bad ones) for the big occasions. He took the man of the match award in the Yorkshire Cup final less than three weeks after his arrival, and but for Brett Kenny, he would surely have won the Lance Todd Trophy at Wembley.

Sterling created many tries with his skilled handling, and his tactical kicking was impeccable, not least when he came back from injury to lead Hull to victory in the Cup replay at Widnes. There was one memorable occasion in the semi-final replay against Castleford when he calmly kicked the ball over his own shoulder for his winger to run on to.

For some weeks he was hampered by stitches above his eye and attempts were made to rest him as substitute but he still took the field to win individual honours. To Hull's credit they were astute enough to use Sterling to spread the code's gospel around the schools and here again he proved an admirable ambassador.

20   There was astonishment in Britain when Peter Sterling failed to claim a Test place against the touring British Lions team in the summer of 1984. When he rejoined Hull early in the 1984–85 season astonishment turned to total disbelief as Sterling again proved the complete Rugby League craftsman. Here he breaks through the Castleford defence in the first Challenge Cup semi-final at Headingley.

Brett Kenny (Wigan)

Brett Kenny's arrival at Wigan was delayed until December by home circumstances but he immediately made up for lost time. The complete professional and a superbly inventive player, Kenny commanded little attention with his appearance on the field but proved once again that he is the ideal link man for any team.

There is a strong feeling in Britain that Australia functions better as a unit with Kenny at stand-off rather than Wally Lewis because of his ability to complete the on-field jigsaw. Kenny's try tally of nineteen was evidence of his ability to take advantage of openings. But the true value of this unassuming Australian was the opportunities he gave to others.

21   A superbly inventive player, Brett Kenny often commanded little attention with his appearance on the field, but proved once again that he is the ideal link-man for any team. Kenny underlined all his skills by his glorious performance for Wigan in the Challenge Cup final at Wembley.

A natural ball-player, Kenny always varied his tactics with rare judgement and the timing of his passes was exceptional. Hints of a defensive weakness proved groundless and he showed copybook tackling. His courage was exemplified in the second round of the Challenge Cup at Warrington, when he twice dived on a loose ball with boots flying round him.

He was mortified when he gave only a modest display, by his standards, in the Challenge Cup semi-final against Hull KR but atonement followed with his glorious virtuoso performance at Wembley that caused him rightly to be hailed as one of the best players in the world.

Mal Meninga (St Helens)

The signing by St Helens of the Australian centre, Mal Meninga, provoked more discussion than any other during the season. His first appearance almost doubled the Knowsley Road attendance and that interest was maintained at fever-pitch for weeks as St Helens embarked on a thirteen-match winning run, starting with Meninga's debut against Castleford.

Frustrating and deceptively casual on occasions, he did not always dominate in bread-and-butter matches but in two major finals he was outstanding. In the Lancashire Cup final at Wigan he scored two blistering tries and collected two more in St Helens's Premiership final victory at Elland Road against Hull Kingston Rovers.

22 Deceptively casual on occasions, the Australian centre Mal Meninga did not always dominate in run-of-the-mill matches for St Helens, but in two major cup finals he was outstanding. In the Lancashire Cup final against Wigan he scored two tries, and collected two more, one of them pictured here, in the final of the Premiership Trophy against Hull KR.

Those tries summed up Meninga's play. His size and strength were accepted features and he showed a rare ability to swat tacklers away. He could also stand his ground like a monument and hold off defenders before passing the ball.

The surprise aspect of his play was his speed. Meninga took surprisingly little time to hit his stride for a big man and was usually in full cry when he took the ball. This was never better shown than in long-range scores in the Premiership semi-final against Wigan, when he ran more than half the length of the field, and in the final against Hull KR, when he took a high interception well and held off acknowledged sprinters over seventy-five yards. His value to Saints can be judged in far more than his twenty-eight tries; Meninga breathed new life into a famous club.

Mark Broadhurst (Hull Kingston Rovers)

Mark Broadhurst is the only forward to be included in my list and earns recognition for the second successive season. Few will dispute that the New Zealand Test prop is one of the best and most consistent players in the game. He has a solid, professional approach to his job and, while always in the thick of the forward action, rarely gets involved in the seamy side of play.

When his side had to clear their lines, Broadhurst was invariably the first to drive the ball in, and he showed an ability to get up in support that spoke volumes for his football knowledge as much as his speed. Broadhurst has a committed approach to the game that is always to be admired and he leads by example. Although scoring only three tries, his attacking prowess was better judged by the number he helped create for others. His subtle touch was never better demonstrated than in the Premiership final, when his quick dummy and equally swift break set up a try for centre Ian Robinson, a simple move perfectly accomplished.

The New Zealander's attitude to the game was well illustrated when he received another of his many man of the match presentations after the club's final home fixture of the season, the Premiership win over Leeds. Broadhurst said, 'You can only get out of the game what you put into it.' In his case that contribution was considerable. Though naturally Rovers were keen to persuade Broadhurst to stay at Craven Park for the 1985–6 season, he has sadly decided to remain in New Zealand.

23 For a second successive season the New Zealand prop Mark Broadhurst has earned recognition in this selection of the five players of the year. He was always in the thick of the action for Hull KR, showing great football knowledge as well as a solidly professional attitude to the game.

6

THE AMATEUR GAME

If there is one thing the amateur game has plenty of, it is cup competitions – at national, county, regional and district levels. So it may seem surprising that the invitation to take part in yet one more knock-out competition should have provided BARLA with the most exciting news of the season. All concerned with rugby league must have been delighted when the Rugby Football League re-opened the gates to professional–amateur matches, and allowed BARLA to enter two teams for the John Player Trophy for the first time since 1980. The two teams were the finalists in the previous season's National Trophy, and that set the scene for the winners, Dudley Hill of Bradford, and the runners-up, Myson's of Hull, to be paired with Keighley and Dewsbury respectively in the preliminary round.

Unfortunately for the amateurs, but much to the relief of the professionals, neither side was able to emulate Cawood's feat against Halifax in 1977 and move through to the next round. At the Boulevard, Myson's, without four regulars because of suspension, gave Dewsbury the fright of their lives before going down 2–8, and at Lawkholme Lane, Dudley Hill overcame the dismissal of hooker John Pitt in the thirty-seventh minute to stage a tremendous fight-back from 2–20 down at half-time to a more respectable 10–24 final score.

Half-backs Albert Hannah and Andy Harland inspired the Bradford side, and the crowd of 1,520, Keighley's best of the season, left the ground full of admiration for the amateurs from the Pennine League. The performances of both BARLA sides should have been more than good enough to convince their critics that they should be allowed to compete in the professionals' major competitions the following season.

Sadly, the amateurs were not included in the Silk Cut Challenge Cup, but that set-back did little to inhibit an otherwise impressive season for BARLA. The standard of rugby reached new heights, the boundaries of the game were further extended, new sides being formed in Cheltenham, Gloucester, Bristol, Sunderland, Newcastle, London and Wales, and plans were drawn up for leagues in the North-east, the South-west and even Cornwall. The existing leagues once again declared increased membership.

The first major events of the season were the county cup competitions, attracting record entries and large attendances while providing plenty of surprises. In the Forshaws Lancashire Cup, fancied sides like Leigh Miners, Mayfield, Simms Cross and Crosfields all fell by the wayside as Waterhead of Oldham overcame Bill Ashurst's Rosebridge, and Blackbrook from St Helens disposed of Woolston in the semi-finals.

It was to be a first BARLA cup final appearance for either side, and in front of 1,100 spectators at Watersheddings, Waterhead, inspired by the man of the match, prop Mick Hough, and loose forward Johnny Morris, took the trophy with a tremendous 18–0 success. Tries from three-quarters Steve O'Brien, Carmel Sealey and Steve Goddard, plus a Chris Hall goal, put the local side in command by 14–0 at half-time. The Blackbrook loose forward, Gary Fletcher, and their scrum-half, Gary Walkden, worked hard to salvage the game, but Waterhead's fourth try from Tony Gallagher ensured victory.

The Fosters Cumbria Cup final proved a thriller, Glasson fighting back from a 2–10 interval deficit to snatch a dramatic 14–10 win ten minutes from time. Ulverston had looked well set for victory when three goals from Peter Dickinson and a try from Jim Salisbury had put them 10 points ahead, but the Cumbrian hooker, Gary Mounsey, led Glasson's remarkable recovery, adding two superb tries to Joe Sullivan's three goals to ensure their success.

Yet surpassing both these wins was the Bass Yorkshire Cup final, when undefeated Jesmond (formerly Beecroft and Wightman) met West Hull in an all-Humberside contest. The first match at the Boulevard was watched by no less than 1,500 spectators. A try from full-back Adrian Hart, goaled by winger Tony Petty, gave West Hull the lead until two minutes from time, when a try from the Jesmond centre, Kenny Lawler, enabled Carl Michaels to equalize with the conversion and secure a replay.

It was two months before the bad weather abated, and then the replay was held at Craven Park. Tries from hookers Billy Mallinson and Lawler plus a goal from Michaels pushed Jesmond into a 10–4 interval lead, but West Hull stormed back to add tries from centres Dave Smart and Wayne Jenkins to the first-half effort of Bernard Brown. Tony Petty's only goal stretched West Hull's winning lead to 14–10, despite playing most of the second half with only twelve men, following the dismissal of prop forward Neil Dawson.

At Youth level, there were first final appearances for Lancashire's Woolston and Crosfield in a contest won by Woolston who had the match winners in centres Mike Stuart and Tony Thornily, who scored the try and the goal for their 6–0 win.

In Cumbria and Yorkshire Glasson and West Hull also won their respective

Youth cups. In the BNFL Cumbria Youth final, the holders, Kells, were Glasson's opponents and defences were well on top throughout. It took two penalty goals from prop Wayne Bowness to one from Kells's full-back, Neil Templeton, to give Glasson a slender 4–2 advantage, leaving Kells without a county cup at any level for the first time since their inception. The winning margin was even less in the Yorkshire Youth final, a solitary drop goal from the man of the match, the Hull centre Paul Eastwood, playing for West Hull, proving sufficient to beat Batley Boys by just 1–0.

By January 1985 it was the turn of the county championships to take priority as the selectors viewed players for the forthcoming annual internationals against France. Once again Lancashire dominated the open-age contest, their rock-solid defence and robust forward play, allied to the deft distributive skills of skipper John Percival at loose forward, and the scrum-half, Gary Walkden, providing a winning combination.

Despite conceding their first try for three seasons, Lancashire still overcame Cumbria 18–8 at Barrow, and the following week, Yorkshire did likewise by 14–4 to give the Cumbrians the wooden spoon. A 'battle of the roses' to decide the destiny of the championship was an exciting prospect, but the actual contest was disappointing as Lancashire won easily by 16–0 to lift their second successive county championship title.

At Under-19 level, Cumbria were the unexpected but thoroughly deserving champions. No one could begrudge them their first championship since BARLA's formation in 1973, and most of the credit must go to the coaches, Peter Smith of Kells and Millom's Roy Jackson, who had the Cumbrian youngsters, captained by Hensingham's prop, Mark Harper, ready to move mountains.

First to go were Lancashire, champions for the past five seasons, three goals and a drop goal from the Hensingham full-back, Brian Tunstall, and a try from the Wath Brow winger, Clive Pink, giving Cumbria their very first triumph over Lancashire by 11–6. Another three goals from Tunstall and a try from Walney's prop, Gary Tees, secured a 10–7 win over Yorkshire, and Cumbria lifted their first county championship.

At international level plans were already under way for an open-age tour of Western Australia as part of that state's anniversary celebrations in the summer of 1986. The forthcoming annual encounters against the French were being treated as tests for players able to make the tour. Weekend training sessions, and a whole series of trial games, made these the best prepared BARLA teams ever to contest the amateur internationals but, to their disappointment, the French were to prove victorious at both levels.

The Youth selectors included a record number of Cumbrians in their squad, but that didn't prevent the French winning 17–6 at Craven Park, Barrow.

109

France fielded the same side that had lost 8–14 to the professional Colts two weeks earlier, and the experience they gained proved decisive against the BARLA Youth team.

Kells's scrum-half, Peter Smith, gave BARLA a deserved lead with a superb try in the twenty-third minute, goaled by Wigan St Patrick's centre, Paul Topping. But despite winning the early exchanges, Britain couldn't increase their lead and in the thirty-sixth minute, the French stand-off, Dominique Espugna, pulled back four points with a try. By the fiftieth minute the entire British front row had had to be reorganized because of injury and a penalty and a drop goal from centre Jean Torres had put France into the lead. The St Anne's second-row forward, Leo Casey, was voted the BARLA Youth player of the year for his outstanding contribution, but Dudley Hill's Sean Sarsfield and Blackbrook's Tony Morrison contributed greatly to a fine rearguard action that prevented the French cementing victory until the dying minutes, when winger Luchési and scrum-half Pech collected tries, one of which Torres goaled for that 17–6 victory.

Two weeks later, on 14 April in Salon de Provence, BARLA again found themselves pitched against formidable opposition for the open-age international, facing a side billed as France 'B', and consisting entirely of players from the French Rugby League's first division. Although the temperature was in the mid-eighties, BARLA never wilted and for the first half-hour they dominated play, the pace of the Jesmond winger, Ray Stead, causing havoc in the French defence as the British forwards, led by Crosfield's prop, John Emson, halted the French pack in their tracks with some bone-crunching tackles.

A fifteenth-minute penalty goal from Leigh Miners' Chris Gaskell gave BARLA an early lead, but in the twenty-ninth minute Mayfield's loose forward, Joe Kershaw, was flattened and the French forward, Perez, was sent to the sin-bin. It proved crucial. Britain's policy of retribution let France off the hook, and when the scrum-half, Georges Alquier, raced in for a try from thirty-five yards and Patrick Alberole added his second goal, the French had realized their visitors' limitations. Their confidence was restored and they never looked back from that 8–2 interval lead.

Despite the promptings of captain and centre Steve Critchenson, of Hull Aces, and Lock Lane's scrum-half, Pete Thaler, selected as BARLA's player of the year, Britain had to rely on five goals from as many attempts by Gaskell to keep them in touch until the French winger, Didier Baccou, raced sixty yards for a spectacular sixty-first-minute touchdown to seal the game. It was a 10–14 defeat, but BARLA could take heart from Britain's play. Sadly, however, the term 'amateur international' is now so loosely applied by the French that the spirit of the fixture has possibly gone for ever.

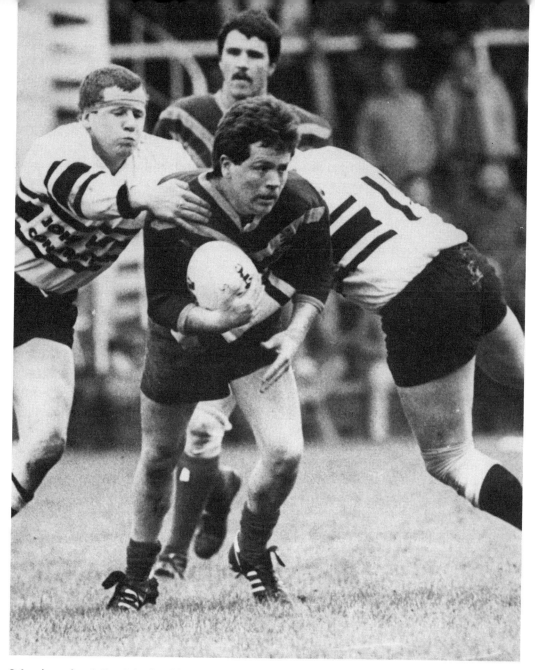

24 Ian Archibald, the West Hull second-row forward, supported by his
prop Roger Sawden, tries to break the Jubilee cover in the final of the
BARLA Whitbread Trophy. Here Archibald is tackled from behind by
Alan Barker who made an important contribution to Jubilee's 26–10
win. This major BARLA competition attracted a record entry of no less
than 141 teams.

At about this time, the Whitbread National Trophy and the major regional league competitions were reaching their final stages, with some powerful new contenders beginning to emerge. The Cumbrians, Egremont, captained by the Great Britain forward, Dave Richardson, won the Cumberland League championship, and then stormed through to the semi-finals of the Whitbread Trophy with brilliant successes against Milford, Dewsbury Celtic and Glasson under their belt.

The Halifax side, Elland, with five Fairbanks brothers, reached the fourth round of the Whitbread Trophy before going down to the holders, Dudley Hill, and then stunned the Pennine League by ending Mayfield's thirteen-year reign as undisputed league champions, taking the premier division championship in their first season after promotion.

In the North-west Counties League, Leigh Miners lost the championship for the first time in five seasons to the brilliant football of the Widnes side, Simms Cross, and the once mighty Pilkingtons were relegated from the premier division. Heworth of York retained the Yorkshire League championship for the third successive season, and Myson's did likewise in the Humberside League, but both were challenged all the way by newly-promoted Yew Tree and Jesmond respectively.

From the record entry of 141 teams, there were team of the year awards for Fitton Hill, London Colonials, South Glamorgan Institute of Higher Education, Oulton, Eccles and Leigh East in the Whitbread Trophy and Leigh East's forward, Brian Burns, became the first player to win three Whitbread's man of the match awards in one season. But against all the odds it was Jubilee of Featherstone and, perhaps inevitably, West Hull who reached the final of the Whitbread Trophy: for the first time the game was played at Headingley.

BARLA Whitbread National Trophy Final
Headingley, Leeds, 19 May
Jubilee (Featherstone) 26   West Hull 10

Sunday 19 May was Jubilee's celebration day, as the Featherstone side ended West Hull's cup dream with a performance that deservedly gave them BARLA's Whitbread Trophy. West Hull had already lifted the Yorkshire Cup, and victories over Simms Cross, Heworth and Millom in earlier rounds had made them favourites to become the first side to win the elusive County and

112

National Cup double. Instead, it was to be the Yorkshire League's senior division champions, Jubilee, who were to carve their own niche in the Cup's history, becoming the first team from outside the premier divisions of the major leagues to land the amateur game's greatest prize. Victories over Dudley Hill and Egremont had already given a clear indication of Jubilee's potential, and under the guidance of the former Featherstone Rovers player, Vince Farrar, they were well prepared for West Hull.

West Hull started impressively; the blistering pace of the Wakefield-bound stand-off, Stuart Wainman, combined with the clever ball distribution of loose forward, Colin Milner, made full use of hooker Ken Jackson's scrum supremacy. A fourteenth-minute penalty from Wainman gave West Hull the lead but, seven minutes later, two tries in a minute were to tip the balance Jubilee's way. A thirty-yard break by their stand-off, Peter Barker, took play deep into the Hull half, and scrum-half Mick Sheldon's perfectly-timed pass sent brother Len storming in under the posts. Within sixty seconds, Len Sheldon had broken clear again, and Mick was on hand to send the second-row forward, Glen Booth, in for a second try, centre Mick Howarth kicking both goals to push West Hull 2–12 adrift. Play was fast and furious, but West Hull hit back with possibly the best try ever seen in the National Trophy final, as Wainman sliced through the cover and side-stepped the full-back in a fifty-yard race to the line, adding the goal points himself.

A further Howarth penalty gave Jubilee a 14–8 interval lead, and he added two more after the restart, Coulson replying with a West Hull penalty. However, Jubilee's prop, Alan Barker, the second-row forwards, Booth and Sheldon, and the ex-professional, Barry Limb, were thriving on the incisive passes of their scrum-half, Mick Sheldon. In the seventieth minute, Wainman broke clear again, but somehow Howarth's outstretched fingers brought down the Humberside stand-off when a score seemed inevitable. It was to prove a crucial tackle as Jubilee at once came back into the attack.

Sheldon's searching up-and-under was misfielded and Barker was on hand to touch the ball firmly down for a third and final Jubilee try, to which Howarth added his seventh goal from eight attempts. Jubilee had the Cup, and Mick Sheldon deservedly took the Wilkinson Sword man of the match award.

The switch of venue from traditional Blackpool had proved a success. A record attendance of over 4,000 had given BARLA record gate receipts. They had enjoyed not only Jubilee's victory but the earlier 16–6 success of Wigan St Patrick's over Leigh Miners in the final of the Youth Trophy, in which a hat-trick of tries from St Patrick's winger, Dave Marshall, had proved decisive.

Jubilee: Smith; Davis, Kellett, Howarth, Ellis; P. Barker, M. Sheldon; Spells, Walker, A. Barker, L. Sheldon, Booth, Limb

Substitutes: Norris for Limb after 52 minutes, Downs for L. Sheldon after 72 minutes

Scorers: tries – L. Sheldon, Booth, P. Barker; goals – Howarth (7)

West Hull: Hart; Petty, Jenkins, Smart, Coulson; Wainman, Baynes; Sawden, Jackson, Brown, Archibald, Card, Milner

Substitutes: Parker for Card after 22 minutes, Bennett for Smart after 64 minutes

Scorers: try – Wainman; goals – Wainman (2), Coulson

Referee: J. Fishwick (Leigh)

Attendance: 4,000

Rugby League in Universities, Polytechnics, Colleges and Upper Schools

---

Cheltenham is not a noted centre of Rugby League football. However, on 3 April, the town staged its second representative game played under the rules of the thirteen-a-side code, when the British Students were defeated 10–18 by their French counterparts at Cheltenham Town's football club ground. The previous occasion on which the town had experienced representative Rugby League occurred in 1908, when the very first touring team to visit Britain, the famous New Zealand 'All Golds', played the final Test of a three-match series against Great Britain, winning 8–5 and taking the series. That great New Zealand team had contained such players as the 'Master', Dally Messenger, the legendary Lance Todd, whose name is commemorated each year at Wembley, and George Smith, one of the initiators of Rugby League in New Zealand.

That early pioneering work in the South-west of England had largely been forgotten until Lionel Hurst, a solicitor who originally hailed from Warrington, came to live in Cheltenham and immediately began to organize a Rugby League club in the town. As part of his promotional work he persuaded the University and College Amateur Rugby League Association (UCARLA) to stage their most important game of the season there. In view of the events of 1908 the executive committee of UCARLA was only too happy to follow in the footsteps of the illustrious pioneers, especially as the local authority in Cheltenham had offered the use of their municipally-owned stadium.

However, that was the point at which controversy, in the shape of the Cheltenham RUFC, intervened. The Union club rented the stadium from the local authority under the terms of a lease which contained a covenant barring the use of the stadium for Rugby League football. Apparently the clause had been inserted at the insistence of the Union club a few years earlier when they had signed the lease, and the local authority had passively accepted the covenant, never dreaming that a request would be made to play League there.

The Cheltenham club flatly refused to overlook the existence of the covenant, and effectively prevented the match from being played at the stadium. But fortunately the local football club, Cheltenham Town, stepped in with an offer to use their facilities at Whaddon Road, and the match went on as scheduled on a cold and wet April evening in front of a few hundred spectators.

British Students v. French Students
Whaddon Road, Cheltenham, 3 April
British Students 10   French Students 18

This was the thirteenth annual encounter between students of the two nations, and the French were defending an impressive record of eleven wins and one draw, with the British team yet to record their first victory. Although rumour suggested that the French might not be as strong as in previous seasons they came into the game with two full internationals in their captain, Dominique Baloup, formerly the captain of the full French Test team, and Daniel Verdes, who was one of the French forwards in the victory against Great Britain at Perpignan earlier in the year. They also had two 'B' internationals in centres Michel Lacroix and Phillipe Lapeyre, and not surprisingly they proved to be formidable opponents.

France took an early 7-point lead in the first fifteen minutes, through a try by Luchési and a conversion and drop goal by Baloup, and the situation looked ominous for the less experienced British team. However, full-back Andrew Bailey, a BARLA international at Under-19 and open-age levels, kept Britain in the game with two brilliant last-ditch tackles on the French winger, Didier

115

Saccareau, and just before half-time Henry Sharp, the Leeds Polytechnic winger, scored a brilliant try in which he showed great pace and elusiveness to beat three defenders to touch down in the corner, a position too difficult for a conversion to be added.

In the second half the game became an exciting tactical battle in difficult muddy conditions, with heavy rain preventing either side from opening up play for the three-quarters. But with only twenty minutes remaining Britain took the lead for the first time when their captain and prop forward, Conal Gallagher, a final-year law student from the University of Hull, broke from sixty yards out, and sprinted for the line to score a thrilling try, converted by Nicholas Johnson, making the score 10–7 to the British Students. At last it appeared that that elusive victory over the French was in sight. The French were visibly shaken, and one sensed that another British score might have sealed the game. However, ten minutes from the end a loose British pass was gratefully received by the French centre, Allengry, who dashed thirty-five yards to score the try which gave his side a 1-point lead. Shortly afterwards Baloup added his second drop goal, and a late try by Luchési, goaled by Hessler, made the game safe for France, though not without a tremendous struggle.

At the post-match banquet the mayor of Cheltenham presented awards to Andrew Bailey and Dominique Baloup, judged to be the outstanding players in their respective sides.

British Students: Bailey (Salford Univ.); Sharp (Leeds Poly.), Melling (Edge Hill College), Elliott (Bradford Univ.), Johnson (Leeds Univ.); Hunter (Wakefield District College), Poynton (Leeds Univ.); Gallagher (Hull Univ.), Proctor (Bradford Univ.), Mellor (Liverpool Poly.), Ellis (Wakefield District College), Rawnsley (Doncaster Inst. of HE), Ragan (De La Salle College of HE)

Scorers: tries – Sharp, Gallagher; goal – Johnson

French Students: Hessler (Toulouse); Lacroix (Toulouse), Lapeyre (Toulouse), Allengry (Toulouse), Saccareau (Toulouse); Ducuing (Bordeaux), Garrigues (Toulouse); Charayron (Toulouse), Scarrazzini (Bordeaux), Dominique Baloup (Bordeaux), Luchési (Marseilles), Verdes (Bordeaux), Bosch (Toulouse)

Scorers: tries – Luchési (2), Allengry; goals – Baloup, Hessler; drop goals – Baloup (2)

Referee: G. Carrière (Béziers)

Earlier in the season the first official Test match had taken place between the students of England and Wales at Central Park, Wigan. The development of Rugby League in Wales among the students of the University Colleges of Swansea and Cardiff and the South Glamorgan Institute of Higher Education has been one of the success stories of the game, and it was felt that the Welsh students were at last ready to take on the English in a match that would carry official status. After twenty minutes a shock result appeared on the cards, with Wales holding a 2-point lead through drop goals by Waring and Rees. However, the English students weathered that early storm and went on to win the game comfortably by 34–6 through tries by Lewis (3), Lenaghan (2), and Melling (2), and three goals by Sean Gallagher, with Wales scoring a late try through Turner.

Officials connected with the student game were impressed by the overall standard of play, and there appears to be a real possibility that a triangular tournament could be established from 1986–87 between the students of England, Wales and France, a development that would surely consolidate the game of Rugby League in Wales at student level and lead to its further development at amateur and possibly professional levels there.

One of the Welsh players who caught the eye at Wigan was centre David Rees, a fresher student from the South Glamorgan Institute. Rees later went on to make a small piece of history by becoming the first player to represent the Welsh students at both codes of rugby.

So that a start could be made with representative rugby, the student sector had been split into four divisions: the English Universities, the British Polytechnics, the English Colleges, and the Welsh Universities and Colleges. Each team played two matches, with the English Universities, the strongest of the sides, beating the Polytechnics 14–6 in Liverpool and defeating the Welsh 44–12 in Cardiff. Not surprisingly players from the Universities' team were the principal contenders for places in the British Students' team later in the year.

The majority of student Rugby League clubs took part during the year in the National Student Merit League, a competition which had been started the previous season to cater for the diversity of the teams involved in UCARLA and the relative brevity of the student season. Altogether twenty-nine teams took part in the Merit League and, subject to having played a minimum of eight games, the top eight teams in the League then competed in a knock-out competition to decide the championship, with the first team playing the eighth, the second against the seventh and so on.

Hull University ended the season with the highest percentage in the Merit League, with Edge Hill College in second place, and both these teams won through to the championship final. Edge Hill College, a teacher training college based at Ormskirk in Lancashire, showed great determination in

25 A Rugby League club was formed at the South Glamorgan Institute of Higher Education, one of the leading physical education centres in Britain, in 1983. Two years later they became the first Welsh team to win a national Rugby League trophy when they defeated by 18–10 Edge Hill College, Ormskirk in the UCARLA Cup final at St Helens. Here their captain and centre, Tony Palmer, scores a crucial second-half try, despite the attentions of two Edge Hill defenders.

defeating Hull 30–18 in an exciting contest, so becoming the first non-university side to win the UCARLA championship in the fifteen years of the competition. This feat was all the more remarkable because Edge Hill were only in their second season as a Rugby League club. They owed much to their captain and British Students' representative, Steve Melling, who proved to be an able organizer and motivator of his fellow students, some of whom had limited experience of the game.

Edge Hill also figured in another major final during the season when they opposed South Glamorgan Institute in the UCARLA Cup final at Knowsley

118

Road, St Helens. For South Glamorgan this was the climax to a remarkable season, and they came to the game determined to become the first club to take a major Rugby League trophy to South Wales. In a pulsating contest the Welsh club were behind at the interval by 8–10, but in the second half they were to last the pace better than Edge Hill and finally ran out victors by 18–10, a try and conversion by Aneurin Emanuel, the brother of David Emanuel who designed the Princess of Wales's wedding-dress, sealing the game with five minutes remaining.

The University match between Oxford and Cambridge had been played annually since 1981 and, with victories in the series standing at two each, the venue for the fifth encounter was to be Headingley, now likely to become the permanent home of this game in the future. The match was played after twenty-four hours of incessant rain, and inevitably the conditions meant that open play would be almost impossible. However, both teams gave a magnificent defensive display and, encouraged by the enthusiastic supporters of both sides, they contrived to produce a game with a thrilling climax.

Going into the last five minutes Cambridge were holding on to a 6–4 lead, having scored a try by John Hall, converted by Steve Windsor-Lewis, in reply to an Oxford try by Craig Marsh, and they seemed to be holding on for victory. However the Oxford president, Andrew Hart, playing in his final varsity match, had other ideas and plunged over the line to score amid scenes of wild jubilation from his team-mates and supporters. Substitute John Risman, the son and grandson of famous Rugby League internationals, missed the kick at goal, but he had already made a small piece of history by becoming the first player to gain a blue at Twickenham and a half-blue at Headingley in the same season, and all done in his first year at Oxford.

In the other major finals Hull University defeated Sheffield University 14–8 in the final of the Universities Athletic Union Championship, thanks to two blockbusting tries by the British Students' captain Conal Gallagher; and Leicester Polytechnic defeated Leeds Polytechnic 17–9 in the final of the British Polytechnics Cup. Leicester were down by 8 points after the first quarter of the game, but they owed much to their full-back and Great Britain Colts international, Robert Whelan, who guided them intelligently and contributed four goals and a drop goal to their win.

It is more than likely that the 1985–86 season will see many new Rugby League clubs being formed at universities, polytechnics and colleges of higher education. It seems possible that the University of Bath, the West London Institute of Higher Education (formerly the Borough Road College), St Paul & St Mary College in Cheltenham, Birmingham Polytechnic and a number of others will be extending even further the boundaries of Rugby League football.

BUSCARLA Open Rugby Magazine Cup Final
Central Park, Wigan, 14 May
Wigan College of Technology 29   St John Rigby College 2

Although fifty-five teams entered the *Open Rugby* Cup during the season the competition was decimated by the effects of the teachers' industrial action, which disrupted school sport and caused some strong schools, including the Cup holders, Cowley School, to withdraw from the competition. However, the two finalists promised to be worthy of the occasion, with St John Rigby College appearing in their fourth successive final (having been the first winners of the Cup in 1982) and their near neighbours, Wigan College of Technology, appearing in their first final.

Although the match was played in incessant rain a good-sized crowd was attracted to Central Park to see the great rivals in action. Despite the conditions neither side appeared to have problems in handling the ball and St John Rigby dominated the game territorially in the early stages, taking the lead from a penalty by Jeff Bimson after twenty minutes. However, the College of Technology were stung into action by this reverse, and, with Paul Topping, a BARLA Under-19 international, prominent they worked a movement which saw Paul Doherty dodging over near the posts for a try which Topping converted.

Early in the second half the strain seemed to tell on Rigby, as Wigan College moved into an invincible lead with tries by David Fell, Martin Coop and Clive Wilson, and two further goals by Topping, to give them a 22–2 lead after twenty minutes of the second half. However, St John Rigby continued to press the Wigan College defence with giant prop forward Ian Tolan repeatedly requiring the attention of three defenders to stop his bullocking runs, and John Booth and Damien Ratchford always prominent.

However, a further 7 points were added for Wigan College through a drop goal and try to Paul Doherty and a conversion by Topping to give them a deserved victory by 29–2, with Doherty being named as the man of the match.

Wigan College of Technology: Jordan; Wilson, Hibbert, Maskery, Coop; Fell, Paul Doherty; Moran, Wilde, Elliot, Oram, Ellis, Topping

Scorers: tries – Paul Doherty (2), Coop, Wilson, Fell; goals – Topping (4); drop goal – Paul Doherty

St John Rigby College: O'Keefe; Tony Doherty, Dey, Stazicker, Lowe; Booth, Bimson; Tolan, Davies, Partington, Ratchford, Gannon, Henry

Scorer: goal – Bimson

Referee: S. Wall (Leigh)

Trevor Hunt (BARLA)
Martyn Sadler (Students' Rugby League)

26   Neil Pickering and Robert Coulson both played for the British Polytechnics representative team. Here they are on opposite sides in the final of the British Polytechnics Cup. Pickering of Leeds Polytechnic is a picture of determination as he carries the ball to Coulson of Leicester Polytechnic. Leicester went on to win the match 17–9 in only their second season, illustrating the expansion of RL at student level.

7

REFLECTIONS

With no incoming or outgoing tours and with all playing activity restricted to the domestic scene, many experienced observers felt that the 1984–85 season would be a quiet one. As in previous years, however, the season provided shocks and unforeseen changes, some of which may affect dramatically the future of British Rugby League.

The most important development was the increase in the number of overseas players, especially from Australia and New Zealand, to join British clubs. No one could have expected that, within two months of the start of the season, no less than seventy-eight foreign players would be registered with British clubs, enough talent to make up six teams. Some critics expressed fears that there would be no room for the emergence of young British stars, that British playing standards generally would drop, and that large sums of money would be taken out of the British game to pay for foreign players' contracts. A close look at the history of Rugby League should have dispelled these fears. Since the early 1900s, when New Zealanders like George Smith and Lance Todd and Australians like Albert Rosenfeld came to this country, to the forties and fifties when Rugby League gave a warm welcome to such outstanding overseas players as Arthur Clues, Cec Mountford, Pat Devery and Lionel Cooper the British game has benefited from the integration of overseas players with their own. Certainly in the forties and fifties the standard of British Test match Rugby League had never been higher.

Because it has been mainly confined to three northern counties for the best part of eighty years, the public now wants to see interesting and colourful personalities from beyond RL's traditional boundaries. In the past, these came mainly from Rugby Union but with that well of talent now drying up and with clubs reluctant to spend big money on untried players the number of signings from Union is now almost non-existent. Consequently attendances at Leeds, Halifax, St Helens and Wigan leapt up as crowds flocked to see the skills

27 The influence of the former New Zealand Test captain, Graeme West, on the younger Wigan players was enormous. Here West deservedly celebrates his man of the match award after a superb display against Hull KR in the semi-final of the Challenge Cup.

of Eric Grothe and Tony Currie at Leeds, Michael Hagan and Ron Ryan at Halifax, Mal Meninga and Phil Vievers at St Helens, and Brett Kenny and John Ferguson at Wigan. They were not disappointed in what they saw. Nor was the management of those clubs when they watched Leeds top the table throughout March and April, St Helens win the Lancashire Cup, Halifax fulfil their aim of retaining first-division status and Wigan return to Wembley to win the 1985 Challenge Cup. Though naturally there were some disappointments and failures, even second-division clubs like Fulham, Salford, and Keighley had their quota of Australians to help in the development of the club's amateurs and young professionals.

28 The blistering pace of the Australian winger John Ferguson, from Eastern Suburbs, was an important factor in Wigan's outstanding season. The play of Henderson Gill, on the left wing, improved out of all recognition when Ferguson joined the club.

The principal effect of the Australian and New Zealand invasion was a sharp increase in the playing standards and levels of fitness of the British players in the clubs which the overseas stars had joined. There is no doubt that at Wigan, for example, the play of Henderson Gill and the youngster Shaun Wane improved out of all recognition when they were joined by the Eastern Suburbs' winger John Ferguson and the ex-Kiwi Test captain Graeme West. At the same time the movement of a number of British players to Australia in the summer of 1985 will enable them to gain vital experience in the Sydney and Brisbane Leagues. Players like Brian Noble, Lee Crooks, Garry Schofield, and Andy Goodway will be better equipped to face the Tests with the New Zealanders this coming autumn after their Australian experience. Though the Rugby League Council has now ruled that the clubs' allowance of foreign players must be reduced from five to three over the next three seasons, I'm sure that most clubs will continue to carry their quota. The only problem is one of staleness, with players competing throughout the year in both hemispheres. Many of our younger players are now totally dependent on the game for their living and pass to and fro between continents in search of lucrative contracts.

Few could have forecast the extent to which the Rugby Football League would become entangled with legal problems during the season. Throughout the summer and early autumn the 'Fulham affair' rumbled through the courts, threatening serious consequences for the club and the game of Rugby League generally. When a group of players, after the old Fulham club had been wound up, sought freedom of contract through their legal advisers, the formation by Roy Close of a new Fulham club began to look a pretty doubtful investment. If the players were to be declared free agents, as they eventually were, then Fulham would be left with no players and a huge capital outlay for the purchase, in Mr Close's words, of 'three bags of kit and several rugby balls'. By November 1984, after Warrington had earned the wrath of all in Rugby League by signing three former Fulham players, Hussein M'Barki, Steve Diamond and David Allen, without any payment to Fulham, the outlook for Rugby League in London looked bleak.

With other Fulham players like Steve Bayliss and Peter Souto seeking their rugby in France and Martin Herdman and Adrian Cambriani searching for other RL clubs in Britain it looked as if the principle of 'freedom of contract' would now be introduced into Rugby League to the detriment, and possible closure, of many of the smaller clubs. Thankfully, with the help of overseas players, amateurs, and ex-players, like Sean Hoare, who returned to the fold, and with the application and dedication of coach Roy Lester and the club's buyers, Mr and Mrs Close, the Fulham club was saved. With other clubs

125

ostracizing the players who had sought freedom of contract and with the players' union realizing that such freedom might well mean fewer clubs and fewer professional players, the heat faded out of the situation.

More controversy, with further threats of legal action, sprang from another spate of unacceptable bullying of the Rugby League by the Rugby Union. However, the publicity given to these new incidents and the near hysteria they caused merely reflected the strength and rapid growth of amateur Rugby League and the many weaknesses, now nakedly exposed, of the Rugby Union.

In the end it was left to myself to challenge the Union rule which had the effect of banning schoolmasters from involvement in schoolboy Rugby Union at all levels if they had had any sort of contact with the professional game. Taking up the cudgels on behalf of others similarly involved, such as Alan McInnes (the Wigan coach), John Bevan (Warrington) and Clive Griffiths (Salford), I threatened to challenge the Union's ruling in the High Court. The outcome was a decision to let us continue to attend meetings of the Lancashire Schools RU committee. Later, the International Board declared that from September 1985 schoolmasters would be allowed to take part in all areas of school rugby of either code.

However, what mattered most in the whole affair was the massive media coverage which the dispute aroused and especially the goodwill earned by Rugby League. This became fertile soil for BARLA for it was Rugby Union's attitude to the rights of the individual amateur RL player which was vilified by the media. Again, the hostility aroused at Cheltenham over the Union club's refusal to allow a British Students' international against France to be played in a council-owned stadium, the outcry over the refusal to select a Union player for a representative squad because he had played amateur Rugby League, the tearing down of posters advertising the Rugby League club at Oxford were all sad incidents. But at least they highlighted the spectacular growth of the game generally during the season and indicated the weaknesses of the opposition when their foolish and mean-spirited regulations are challenged.

If BARLA maintains its pressure on the Union code and insists that an amateur player be given complete freedom of access to either code at any time then the battles of the 1984–85 season will be seen as marking the beginning of a truly national sport, at least at amateur level. The amateur code can look forward to a healthy future with only one cloud on the horizon – ironically a restrictive practice perpetrated by Rugby League itself at senior level. The inclusion of two amateur clubs, Dudley Hill and Myson's, in the preliminary round of the John Player Special Trophy in 1984–85 was a forward-looking step by the League's officers, but the omission of amateurs from the Silk Cut

Challenge Cup was a backward move. I think BARLA should be allowed twelve teams in the preliminary round alongside the twenty second-division sides, and those twelve teams should reflect the growth of the game in London, South Wales, the Midlands and the South-west as well as in the traditional areas of the North. The interest kindled in new territory would be considerable and the additional media coverage could only help to spread the game further.

The new season saw the birth of two new clubs, Mansfield Marksman and Sheffield Eagles. This increase to thirty-six professional clubs meant further reorganization of the numbers in the two divisions, sixteen in the first and twenty in the second division being agreed upon. However, that all twenty second-division clubs managed to complete the season was a close-run affair, for both Southend Invicta and Bridgend were to show how precariously balanced has been the expansion of Rugby League in the eighties. For Invicta, the move from Maidstone to Southend was fraught with boardroom difficulties which were brought to a head as support declined from a reported average of 1,000 at Maidstone to something approaching 150 at Southend. Though credit must be given to a gallant band of Southend players, coaches, and enthusiasts who just managed to keep the flag flying, one has to ask why second-division clubs cannot carry a majority of amateur players on their books supported simply by two, three or perhaps four professionals.

Bridgend's problems were of a different kind. The club's move from Cardiff, brought about by the death of their financial backer, saw the loss of many players who should have been an attraction to the Welsh public and who now, after three years, were reasonably experienced in the League game. The club could not carry the loss of such as Tommy David, Steve Fenwick, Brynmor Williams and Lynn Hallett, who left the club for various reasons before the start of the season. The age-old dilemma of trying to find a Welsh side good enough to attract an interested but critical Welsh public began again, though this time progress was hindered by a lack of understanding between the professional club and the organizers of the healthy Welsh amateur league. So Bridgend, like Cardiff, almost stumbled to a halt; unable to win more than one match the whole season, crowds rarely rose above the 350 mark.

Fulham's problems, mentioned earlier, were increased by the unsuitability of their new home at the Crystal Palace national recreation centre. Their gates, too, dropped alarmingly. One hopes that a move to the Central London Polytechnic ground at Chiswick will give them larger and more stable support.

Carlisle was the one new club which did begin to prosper. On the field, they figured throughout the season in the race for promotion and off the field began to lay the foundations of a successful professional club. An amateur league was formed in the area, an Alliance League side was built up and played at Penrith, thereby creating another area of interest to help the parent club. Youth and schools rugby were encouraged. A social club as a source of revenue was set up. Attendances, still disappointing, will surely begin to grow on such foundations.

Despite the failure of the two new entrants, Mansfield Marksman and Sheffield Eagles, to attract gates much above the 1,000 mark, it's good to record that in their own areas both clubs are laying the same sort of foundations as Carlisle. Both have well-run social clubs, both foster amateur and youth rugby in the surrounding districts, and both have a fresh approach to the marketing of Rugby League as was demonstrated by their Easter weekend of rugby which saw both clubs playing Roanne, from France, and saw Mansfield journey to Perpignan to play the Catalan XIII.

It is useless to give a community uneducated in Rugby League a professional club without amateur development preceding it and without any attempt to bring the game to the schools. This is where Rugby League's development resources should be channelled. Only when amateur and youth sections are flourishing, when sufficient local interest has been generated to support an open-age amateur league, should we seriously think of forming a professional club in the area.

A feature of the second division which especially pleased me was a decline in the number of fading, ageing players who once earned a decent living for a minimum of effort. Many clubs now look to youngsters emerging from BARLA and, at less expense, they gained much from their services during the season, not only in fitness and attitude but also in performance. Salford and Swinton certainly gave youth its chance and probably gained promotion because of it, while a club like Runcorn Highfield made the move from Huyton without many of their older players. With the acquisition of such young half-backs as Blythin and Garrity, Runcorn had their best season for years. Many new faces were also given their chance in the newly-formed Alliance League, one of the success stories of the season. Formed from the old Lancashire and Yorkshire 'A' team Leagues, the Alliance was made up of any clubs wanting to provide competition for their reserve team. The number of reserve teams taking part meant that regular fixtures could at last be maintained, serious competition could be fostered and crowd interest sustained. Such support was to top the 2,000 mark at Wigan with four-figure crowds also at Leeds, St Helens, Hull and elsewhere. Youngsters, trialists, anyone of promise, could at last gain regular experience from a competition which was meaningful. It was significant that it was not only the major clubs who were successful: second-division clubs like Salford and Swinton also recorded good attendances and regular victories.

Despite the unsuccessful tour by the Rugby League Lions to Australia and New Zealand in 1984, and Britain's annihilation by Australia in 1982, by the end of the 1984–85 season I began to believe that the health of the professional game in Britain was better than for some years. Over two-thirds of the league clubs won a rise in attendances, and it says much for Rugby League that in the present harsh economic climate of the north an aggregate crowd of over 50,000 could be drawn to the two county cup finals. And when the two St Helens v Wigan league matches can attract a total attendance of 40,000 there is plenty of evidence that, given the quality of the players, the crowds will come.

In the league programme, the Wigan match against Hull KR, and St Helens's matches against Hull and Leeds, would rank with any such contests of the past, while the various cup competitions provided some spectacular rugby. The two county cup finals, dominated by the Australians Mal Meninga (St Helens) and Peter Sterling (Hull), were absorbing contests, as was the final of the John

29   Deryck Fox, Featherstone Rovers' scrum-half, was one of the outstanding young players of the 1984–85 season and deservedly won caps at full and Under-21 levels against France. Here he makes a determined break through the French defence in the first Test against France.

Player Special Trophy between Hull and Hull KR. The Silk Cut Challenge Cup final between Wigan and Hull was a memorable occasion but the previous rounds also witnessed contests of the highest quality, especially the Widnes third-round replay against Hull in the Challenge Cup and the two semi-finals in the same competition.

The emphasis on attacking play, now encouraged by the sixth-tackle turnover rule, allows players of the calibre of Ellery Hanley, Gary Prohm, Henderson Gill, John Ferguson and Mick Burke to demonstrate their skills. Two in particular, Hanley and Prohm, took advantage of the new opportunities to run with the ball to reap a harvest of tries. Prohm's forty-five tries were a testimony to his strength and eye for an opening while Hanley's fifty-five tries were a combination of his own special magical qualities. As Hanley raced ahead in the scoring charts in his attempt to beat the fifty-try barrier, last broken by Billy Boston twenty-three years ago, he displayed not only speed, strength, and footballing skills but a knack of doing the unexpected. His ability to receive the ball, standing still in midfield, and to spurt suddenly through a gap in the opposition stemmed from supreme confidence in his own ability. Here was the outstanding entertainer of the 1984–85 season. Of the youngsters, Shaun Edwards (Wigan), Deryck Fox (Featherstone Rovers), David Creasser (Leeds) and Gary Divorty (Hull) also had their moments.

In terms of defence, I thought we made little progress during the season and the tackling in far too many games merely reflected the same unsatisfactory state of affairs highlighted by the Australian touring side in 1982. A further indication of the decline in the art of tackling was the prevalence of head-high tackles, which plagued far too many matches. It was significant that, in a 'tackle of the month' competition, the prizes were won mostly by overseas players like Phil Vievers, Kurt Sorensen and Michael Hagan. Much work remains to be done here: it is inexcusable that some first-division sides never once in a full season hold a tackle practice session. I certainly don't want to see the British game become as defence-orientated as it is in, say, Sydney, but I do think the Australians have much to teach us about this aspect of the game. The Halifax defence in the John Player matches against St Helens and Hull KR provided a lesson in solid tackling, but sadly the principal exponents, Bella, Neller, Ryan, Hagan, and Langmack, were all Australians.

There is no doubt that the sixth-tackle turnover rule accelerated changes in the game during the season. A greater appreciation of the need to open out play through running and handling skills, with less reliance on boring, stereotyped forward drives down the middle of the field, has brought greater movement of the ball between the two sides. The forwards need to be fitter and faster and, in the main, they proved to be so. The increase in broken play resulting from kicks upfield created more space to be exploited by the backs. Hence the dominant role of big centres, like Hanley, Prohm and Meninga, in the scoring charts. This amount of broken play, accompanied by considerable midfield running, allowed the scrum-half to come more into his own as the season progressed.

30   Paul Harkin, the Hull KR scrum-half, made a welcome return to the side after an early-season injury to Gordon Smith. Harkin's skill and hard work gained him a place in the Great Britain squad.

31   George Fairbairn, the Hull KR full-back, rarely hesitates to join in attacking moves by his three-quarters. Here he breaks through the Hull defence, despite the attentions of Crooks and Evans, in the final of the John Player Special Trophy.

Released somewhat from his role at the base of the scrum, the scrum-half is now the key contributor in a side. It is no coincidence that scrum-halves invariably collect the man of the match award in the major sponsored games and the skill and hard work of such as Peter Sterling (Hull), Michael Ford (Wigan), Paul Harkin (Hull KR) and Michael Hagan (Halifax) brought them their deserved nominations. Though there are now fewer scrums as a result of the turnover rule, the scrum-half's workload has been increased in open play.

The role of the full-back, too, is changing, with the emphasis now on his ability to mount attacks once the ball has been retrieved from the opposition's kick upfield. Speed is now one of the main priorities for a full-back and here Gary Kemble (Hull) was to exploit that gift against any opposition. George Fairbairn (Hull KR), Mick Burke (Widnes), and Phil Vievers (St Helens) offered many examples of the need for the full-back to be constantly alert for gaps in the opposing defence and to link up in attack if the ball had been fielded by one of his colleagues. In defence, too, there was another major change for full-backs to master, apparent as teams encouraged the use of the 'up-and-under' or 'bomb' kick following the sixth tackle. It is now essential for a full-back to have the catching ability and courage to withstand these high kicks, usually taken in dangerous positions round his try-line. It is no accident that the best practitioners of this skill were Fairbairn, Burke, and Vievers – all ex-Rugby Union players and trained in the skill of fielding a long high kick.

However, the most dramatic change of all was surely in that of loose forward play. Here the Great Britain coach, Maurice Bamford, searched far and wide for a loose forward good enough to play against the New Zealand Test team next season and it is significant that of the three chosen for squad training in the summer only Harry Pinner (St Helens) is an old-style creative loose forward, skilled in ball handling. The other two, Gary Divorty (Hull) and Chris Arkwright (St Helens), are noted for their running skills, though Divorty is also a good ball-handler. Arkwright, of course, normally plays at stand-off. The rapid decrease in the number of scrums per match now puts less emphasis on a loose forward's ball-playing skills in conjunction with an attacking scrum-half. The need for a side to carry the ball through only six tackles has also meant less demand for the precision passing and sleight of hand that were required of the number 13 in the days of unlimited tackles. The dominant position in world Rugby League of such loose forwards as Pearce (Australia) and McGahan (New Zealand) underlines the present trend in Britain for fast-covering players, able to tackle and able to break up the opposition in strong surging runs but with no great emphasis on handling ability and constructive play. It's a trend I regret.

On the whole, I was heartened by what I saw on the field during the 1984–85 season and thought that the game was becoming more and more attractive to watch. Changes in tactics, attitudes, and playing roles were, I think, welcomed by the majority of spectators. They might well think that 1984–85 was the season when the British Rugby League giant stirred in his sleep. It will be our failure if by the 1990s the giant is not fully awake.

Ray French

Appendix 1

THE JOHN PLAYER SPECIAL TROPHY

Preliminary round

Hunslet 2
Workington T. 6

Carlisle 8
Bradford N. 26

Keighley 24
Dudley Hill 10

Myson's 2
Dewsbury 8

Sheffield E. 17
Wakefield T. 6

Bramley 20
Southend I. 6

1st round

Hull KR 32
Leigh 5

Rochdale H. 10
Mansfield M. 8

Workington T. 12
Widnes 22

Featherstone R. 17
Barrow 12

Bradford N. 22
Swinton 1

St Helens 60
Keighley 8

Warrington 5
Halifax 17

Castleford 42
Bridgend 4

Dewsbury 14
Salford 8

Runcorn H. 18
Batley 5

Fulham 14
Hull 36

York 6
Oldham 22

Leeds 50
Sheffield E. 2

Wigan 50
Huddersfield 6

Bramley 12
Blackpool B. 10

Whitehaven 64
Doncaster 0

2nd round

Hull KR 34
Rochdale H. 12

Widnes 28
Featherstone R. 10

Bradford N. 12
St Helens 12
(replay: 24–10 to St Helens)

Halifax 20
Castleford 18

Dewsbury 31
Runcorn H. 16

Hull 26
Oldham 14

Leeds 10
Wigan 4

Bramley 33
Whitehaven 5

134

The John Player Special Trophy

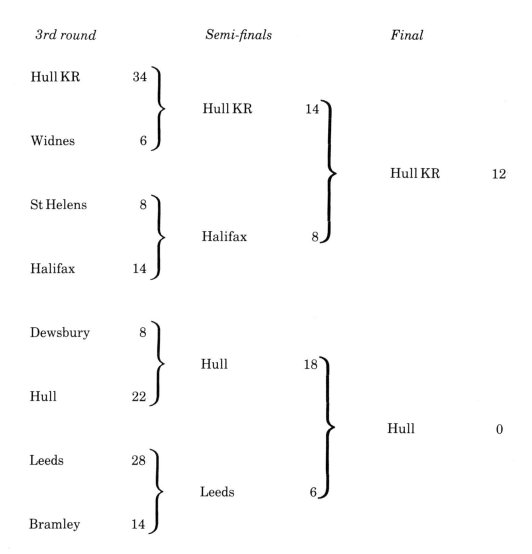

3rd round		Semi-finals		Final	
Hull KR	34				
		Hull KR	14		
Widnes	6				
				Hull KR	12
St Helens	8				
		Halifax	8		
Halifax	14				
Dewsbury	8				
		Hull	18		
Hull	22				
				Hull	0
Leeds	28				
		Leeds	6		
Bramley	14				

Appendix 2

THE PHILIPS VIDEO YORKSHIRE CUP

1st round		*2nd round*		*Semi-finals*		*Final*	
York	20	York	8	Hull	24	Hull	29
Hunslet	16	Hull	38				
Hull	30						
Halifax	10						
Wakefield T.	0	Bradford N.	4	Leeds	1		
Bradford N.	30	Leeds	10				
Castleford	14						
Leeds	16						
Featherstone R.	18	Featherstone R.	18	Featherstone R.	2	Hull KR	12
Batley	17	Bramley	2				
Dewsbury	4						
Bramley	12						
Doncaster	4	Hull KR	18	Hull KR	22		
Hull KR	48	Huddersfield	2				
Huddersfield	9						
Keighley	6						

136

Appendix 3

THE BURTONWOOD BREWERY LANCASHIRE CUP

1st round		*2nd round*		*Semi-finals*		*Final*	
Barrow	38	Barrow	10				
Carlisle	4			St Helens	31		
St Helens	58	St Helens	26				
Runcorn H.	14					St Helens	26
Workington T.	0	Rochdale H.	10				
Rochdale H.	11			Leigh	10		
Leigh	22	Leigh	22				
Warrington	14						
Salford	19	Salford	15				
Whitehaven	14			Salford	8		
Oldham	26	Blackpool B.	6				
Blackpool B.	32					Wigan	18
Fulham	18	Swinton	6				
Swinton	25			Wigan	19		
Wigan	28	Wigan	32				
Widnes	8						

Appendix 4

THE SILK CUT CHALLENGE CUP

Preliminary round		*1st round*		*2nd round*	
		Bradford N.	50		
		Southend I.	18	Bradford N.	13
Doncaster	6	Whitehaven	8		
Wakefield T.	25	Wakefield T.	10	Wakefield T.	2
		Sheffield E.	19		
		Warrington	54	Warrington	14
		Wigan	46		
		Batley	8	Wigan	24
		Leigh	14		
		Huddersfield	6	Leigh	27
		Mansfield M.	10		
		Hunslet	34	Hunslet	28
		Rochdale H.	11		
		York	5	Rochdale H.	4
		St Helens	3		
		Hull KR	8	Hull KR	38
Barrow	12	Fulham	4		
Halifax	26	Halifax	17	Halifax	6
		Hull	52		
		Carlisle	6	Hull	22
Leeds	68	Leeds	4		
Bridgend	6	Widnes	14	Widnes	36
		Keighley	5		
		Runcorn H.	12	Runcorn H.	11
		Oldham	8		
		Castleford	14	Castleford	64
		Workington T.	28		
		Dewsbury	6	Workington T.	4
		Bramley	16		
		Blackpool B.	15	Bramley	24
Salford	14	Salford	31		
Featherstone R.	6	Swinton	6	Salford	10

3rd round   *Semi-finals*   *Final*

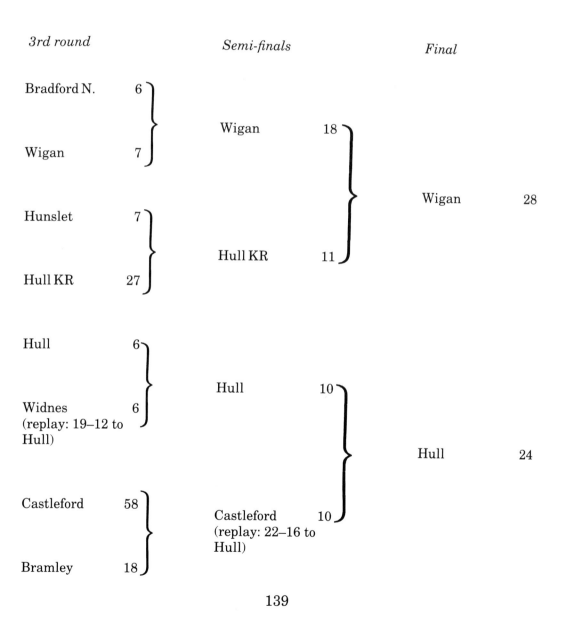

Bradford N.   6

                              Wigan   18

Wigan   7

                                                          Wigan   28

Hunslet   7

                              Hull KR   11

Hull KR   27

Hull   6

                              Hull   10

Widnes   6
(replay: 19–12 to
Hull)
                                                          Hull   24

Castleford   58

                              Castleford   10
                              (replay: 22–16 to
                              Hull)

Bramley   18

Appendix 5

THE SLALOM LAGER CHAMPIONSHIP FINAL LEAGUE TABLES

Division 1

	P	W	L	D	F	A	Pts
Hull Kingston Rovers	30	24	6	–	778	391	48
St Helens	30	22	7	1	920	508	45
Wigan	30	21	8	1	720	459	43
Leeds	30	20	9	1	650	377	41
Oldham	30	18	11	1	563	439	37
Hull	30	17	12	1	733	550	35
Widnes	30	17	13	—	580	517	34
Bradford Northern	30	16	13	1	600	500	33
Featherstone Rovers	30	15	15	–	461	475	30
Halifax	30	12	16	2	513	565	26
Warrington	30	13	17	–	530	620	26
Castleford	30	12	17	1	552	518	25
Barrow	30	9	20	1	483	843	19
Leigh	30	8	20	2	549	743	18
Hunslet	30	7	22	1	463	952	15
Workington Town	30	2	27	1	297	935	5

The F and A columns are headed "Points".

Division 2

	P	W	L	D	Points F	A	Pts
Swinton	28	24	3	1	727	343	49
Salford	28	20	5	3	787	333	43
York	28	21	6	1	717	430	43
Dewsbury	28	21	6	1	539	320	43
Carlisle	28	19	9	–	558	426	38
Whitehaven	28	16	9	3	498	385	35
Batley	28	17	11	–	489	402	34
Fulham	28	16	11	1	521	526	33
Mansfield Marksman	28	15	13	–	525	398	30
Blackpool Borough	28	15	13	–	486	434	30
Wakefield Trinity	28	12	14	2	450	459	26
Rochdale Hornets	28	12	14	2	436	466	26
Huddersfield	28	12	15	1	476	476	25
Runcorn Highfield	28	11	16	1	462	538	23
Keighley	28	11	17	–	484	578	22
Bramley	28	9	17	2	439	492	20
Sheffield Eagles	28	8	20	–	424	582	16
Doncaster	28	6	20	2	353	730	14
Southend Invicta	28	4	24	–	347	690	8
Bridgend	28	1	27	–	258	966	2

141

Appendix 6

THE SLALOM LAGER PREMIERSHIP TROPHY

1st round		*Semi-finals*		*Final*	
St Helens	26	St Helens	37		
Widnes	2			St Helens	36
Wigan	46	Wigan	14		
Hull	12				
Hull KR	42	Hull KR	15		
Bradford N.	18			Hull KR	16
Leeds	36	Leeds	14		
Oldham	18				

Appendix 7

LEADING SCORERS

Tries			*Goals*	
Hanley (Bradford N.)	55		Day (St Helens)	157
Prohm (Hull KR)	45		Fairbairn (Hull KR)	141
Gill (Wigan)	34		Wood (Runcorn H.)	126
Ledger (St Helens)	30		Steadman (York)	122
Meninga (St Helens)	28		Griffiths (Salford)	118
Gribbin (Whitehaven)	27		Parrish (Oldham)	117
Gibson (Batley)	26		Schofield (Hull)	105
Peacham (Carlisle)	25		Creasser (Leeds)	102
Byrne (Salford)	25		Agar (Halifax)	87
Evans (Hull)	24		Jones (Swinton)	87
Ferguson (Wigan)	24			

Points

	Trs	*Gls*	*Dr.Gls*	*Pts*
Day (St Helens)	12	157	–	362
Steadman (York)	20	116	6	318
Fairbairn (Hull KR)	10	135	6	316
Griffiths (Salford)	18	112	6	302
Schofield (Hull)	23	104	1	301

The publication of this book has been made possible
through the generosity of Shopacheck Financial Services Ltd,
6 Wolfreton Drive, Springfield Way, Anlaby, Hull.